A
Tokyo
Romance

A
Tokyo
Romance

a memoir

IAN BURUMA

Atlantic Books
London

First published in the United States of America in 2018 by The Penguin Press,
a member of Penguin Group (USA) LLC.

First published in Great Britain in 2018 by Atlantic Books,
an imprint of Atlantic Books Ltd.

1 2 3 4 5 6 7 8 9

A CIP catalogue record for this book is available from the British Library.

Hardback ISBN: 978-1-78239-799-1
Trade paperback ISBN: 978-1-78239-800-4
E-book ISBN: 978-1-78239-801-1
Paperback ISBN: 978-1-78239-802-8

Photographs by the author

Designed by Amanda Dewey

Printed in Great Britain by Bell and Bain Ltd, Glasgow

Atlantic Books
An Imprint of Atlantic Books Ltd
Ormond House
26–27 Boswell Street
London
WC1N 3JZ

www.atlantic-books.co.uk

In memory of Donald Richie, Norman Yonemoto,
and Terayama Shuji

Cultural initiation entails metamorphosis, and we cannot learn any foreign values if we do not accept the risk of being transformed by what we learn.

—Simon Leys, *The Hall of Uselessness,*
New York: NYRB, 2011

A
Tokyo
Romance

ONE

The last thing he said to me, before I closed the door of his smartly decorated loft apartment in Amsterdam, was to stay away from Donald Richie's crowd. This was in the summer of 1975. I can't remember the name of the man who offered this advice, but I have a vague memory of what he looked like: close-cropped gray hair, hawkish nose, an elegant cotton or linen jacket; midsixties, I guessed, a designer perhaps, or a retired advertising executive. He had lived in Japan for some years, before retiring in Amsterdam.

Donald Richie introduced Japanese cinema to the West. I knew that much about him. That he was also a novelist, the author of a famous book about traveling around the Japanese Inland Sea, much praised by Christopher Isherwood, and the director of short films that had become classics of the 1960s Japanese avant-garde I didn't know. But I had read two of his books on Japanese movies and was instantly drawn to the tone of his prose: witty, in a wry, detached way, and polished without being arch or prissy. Reading Richie made me want to meet him, always a perilous step for a fan that can easily end in sharp disillusion.

There was not much biographical information on the covers of his books, but his 1971 introduction to *Japanese Cinema* was written in New York, so I assumed that he was an American.

In any case, I was still in Amsterdam, and Richie was, so far as I knew, in the United States, or possibly in Japan, where I was bound in a month or two, for the first time in my life. My Pakistan International Airlines ticket had been booked. My place at the film department of Nihon University College of Art in Tokyo was secure, as was the Japanese government scholarship that would pay for my living expenses. The thought of moving to Tokyo for several years was intensely exciting but alarming too. Would I be isolated and homesick and spend much of my time writing to people six thousand miles away? Would I come back in a few months, humiliated by moral defeat? I had a Japanese girlfriend named Sumie, who would move to Japan as well, but still.

One of the most appealing features of Richie's books on Japanese cinema was the way he used the movies to describe so much else about Japanese life. You got a vivid idea of what people were like over there, how they behaved in love, or in anger, their bittersweet resignation in the face of the unavoidable, their sense of humor, their sensitivity to the transience of things, the tension between personal desires and public obligations, and so on.

Richie's fond picture of Japan through its movies was not particularly exotic. But then exoticism had never been Japan's main attraction to me anyway. Nor was I interested in traditional pursuits like Zen Buddhism, or tea ceremonies, let alone the rigors of the martial arts. The imaginary characters in the movies described by Richie seemed recognizably human, more human indeed than characters in most American or even European films I had seen. Or maybe it was the common humanity of figures in an unfamiliar setting that made it seem that way. Perhaps that is what excited me most about Japan, which was still no more than an idea, an image in my mind: the cultural strangeness mixed with that sense of raw humanity that I got from the movies, some of which I had seen in art houses in Amsterdam and London, or at the Paris Cinémathèque française, and some of which I had only read about in Donald Richie's books.

I actually stumbled into Japan by accident. Asian culture had played no part in my childhood in Holland, even though The Hague, my hometown, still had a nostalgic whiff of "the Orient," since people returning from the East Indian colonies used to retire there in large nineteenth-century mansions near the sea, complaining of the cold and damp climate, missing the easy life, the clubs, the tropical landscapes, and the servants. I liked Indonesian food, one of the few reminders of the recent colonial past, and the peculiar Indo-Dutch variety of Chinese cuisine: fat oversized spring rolls, thick and oily fried noodles with a fiery Indonesian *sambal* sauce made of chilies and garlic, the delicacy of the original coarsened by the greed of northern European appetites. My father's elder sister had the misfortune of being sent out to the Dutch East Indies as a nanny just before World War II; she ended up spending most of her time in a particularly grim Japanese POW camp. So no nostalgia there.

Asia meant very little to me. But ever since I can remember I dreamed of leaving the safe and slightly dull surroundings of my upper-middle-class childhood, a world of garden sprinklers, club ties, bridge parties, and the sound of tennis balls in summer.

As a child, I was fascinated by the story of Aladdin, rubbing his magic lamp. It is possible that the mix of enchanted travels and faraway lands (he lived in an unspecified city in China) left a mark. The Hague was in any case not where I intended to end up.

Perhaps I was prejudiced from an early age against my native country. My mother was British, born in London, the eldest daughter in a highly cultured Anglo-German-Jewish family, which in my provincial eyes seemed immensely sophisticated. My uncle, John Schlesinger, whom I adored, was a well-known film director. He was also openly gay, and his milieu of actors, artists, and musicians added further spice to the air of refinement I soaked up vicariously. Like many artists, John was both self-absorbed and open to new sensations, anything that stirred his imagination. He wanted to be amused, surprised, stimulated. And so I was always eager to impress, giving a performance of one kind or another, mimicking mannerisms, styles of dress, or opinions that I thought might spark his interest. Of course, despite the posturing, I never felt I was being interesting enough. And recalling my efforts in retrospect is more than a little embarrassing.

But in fact performance came naturally to me. I grew up with two cultures: lapsed Dutch Protestant on my father's side, assimilated Anglo-Jewish on my mother's. I could "pass" in both, but never felt naturally at ease in either. My destiny was to be half in, half out—of almost anything. Passing was my default state. In the meantime, there was never any doubt in my mind that glamour was always somewhere else, in London, especially in my uncle's house, when I was still living in Holland, but preferably somewhere farther afield, where I didn't have to choose.

By the time I was finally liberated from school and set out to live for a year in London, being "into Asia" had become a fashionable attitude: hippie trips to India in a Volkswagen bus, a superficial acquaintance with Ravi Shankar's sitar music, the cloying smell of joss sticks in tea shops selling hash paraphernalia and Tibetan trinkets. I got to know some Indian hippies in England, who made the most of their mysterious Eastern provenance and were far more successful with impressionable European women than I could ever have hoped to be. One of them, an Assamese Christian from Bangalore, named Michael, was as much of a performer as I was, and he used his exotic allure to the fullest advantage.

The first Japanese I ever met weren't even really Japanese. In 1971, instead of heading east in a Volkswagen bus before settling down to study at university, I traveled west, to California. I was nineteen. I stayed at the house of a friend of my uncle's in Los Angeles, an alcoholic brain surgeon (his hands were steady during operations, I was told). He introduced me to an intense young man named Norman Yonemoto. Slim, tall, with large myopic eyes, which bulged alarmingly when he got excited, Norman bore some resemblance to Peter Lorre, the German actor, in his role as Mr. Moto, the Japanese detective. Like so many young men who drifted to LA, Norman had movie ambitions. For the time being he was making gay porno films. The money was OK. But Norman took gay porno seriously. He was an artist.

Norman was a third-generation Japanese American, raised

in what is now Silicon Valley, where his parents cultivated flowers. There was no talk about Japan, however, when Norman
acted as my guide in Los Angeles, zooming around the freeways
in his silver Volkswagen Beetle, usually in the company of Nick,
his Nordic-looking boyfriend. We cruised along Santa Monica
Boulevard, where handsome young hustlers who hadn't made
it into the movies hung back casually against parked cars, scan-
ning the road for a pickup. We went downtown at night, where
Mexican girls were paid by the dance in dark halls with broken
neon lights. Transvestites trawled for drunken truck drivers in
menacing little bars stuck behind the once glamorous art deco
movie houses. The alcoholic brain surgeon took us to a minia-
ture Western town, a kind of erotic theme park, named Dude
City, with saloons entered through swinging doors, where naked boys in cowboy boots danced on the bar tops. An olive-
skinned young man in a white T-shirt kissed me on the lips.
The surgeon chuckled and whispered that he was Taiwanese.

This was Norman's world, and it seemed a very long way
from Japan. I was in a state of fascinated culture shock: Southern California was more exotic to me than any place I had ever
seen, or would yet see in later years, stranger in its way to European eyes than Calcutta, Shanghai, or Tokyo. Whatever vestiges
of a disjointed Japanese upbringing Norman might still have
had up in the flower gardens of Santa Clara County, they had
long been shed in favor of his California dream of rough sex and
making movies. He embraced LA in all its tawdry glamour.

Rough sex was not for me. The kiss from the Taiwanese was
as far as it went at Dude City. My sexual life at that stage had
consisted of some fumbling affairs with a number of girls, and

a few boys. Most of what I knew I had learned from a more experienced girl from Stuttgart with long blond hair and a Walküre figure who had taken me in hand in London with immense tact and tenderness. But what I lacked in real experience, I made up for in knowingness. Hanging out in gay bars, cruising downtown LA, seeing things I had never seen before, brought me a little closer, I thought, to the sophistication that I associated with my uncle and his friends. It was also very far away from the garden sprinklers of The Hague, which was perhaps the main point.

Norman's younger brother Bruce, who joined us one day from Berkeley, where he was studying art, was rather different. Like me, still searching for his sexual orientation, Bruce was more political than his brother, quicker to pick an argument; he was "into" French theorists. Paris, albeit just in the mind, was his intellectual center, more than LA. Unlike Norman, Bruce was also interested in Japan. This emerged one night when the three of us did a rather conventional thing for the time: we went to Disneyland, in the heart of Orange County, after sharing a tab of LSD.

My memories of that night are still vivid, even though jumbled up in a bit of a blur: The Supremes performed on a gilded stage, changing glittering costumes after every song—that, at any rate, is how I remember it. Norman's eyes shone as he discoursed on the Southern Californian scene while pointing at the childlike caricatures of other cultures displayed in a ride named It's a Small World. In my jacked-up mental state I kept wondering what it all meant, which led to feverish discussions about the meaning of "it."

Compared with Norman's wide-eyed animation, Bruce's soft round face, a little like a painting of a Japanese Buddha, betrayed little. But something in our acid-fueled experience of this Californian fantasy world sparked an argument about identity, less about the meaning of "it" than about who we were and where we came from. "We are Americans," cried Norman in a state of great agitation. "We get to make ourselves over. We can be whatever we want." Whereupon Bruce said: "What about thousands of years of Japanese culture? All that can't just disappear. Anyway, when whites look at us, they don't see Americans, they see Asians. We're Asians, whether we like it or not."

There was nothing much I could contribute to this discussion. And perhaps not too much should be made of these earnest attempts at self-definition. But I like to think that on that night, somewhere between the Pirates of the Caribbean and the Jungle Cruise, a seed of my future orientation toward Japan was planted. For it was not long after that, back in Holland, that I had to make up my mind what to study at university. I tried the law for a month or two before deciding it was not for me. I had already dabbled in art history, at the Courtauld Institute in London, where I worked in the picture library and attended lectures on Picasso by the art historian and former Soviet spy Anthony Blunt. One day, while I was studying a picture of a Joan Miró painting, I felt the stale breath of a man leaning over my shoulder, who exclaimed: "Is that art?" A burly figure in a tweed jacket, he was an expert in medieval English church foundations. I concluded that art history wasn't really for me either.

And so I plumped for Chinese. It was different, it sounded

glamorous, it might be useful one day, I liked Chinese food, and possibly lodged somewhere in the back of my mind were memories of Aladdin, Disneyland, or that Taiwanese boy in Dude City.

This was in 1971. China was still in the last throes of the Cultural Revolution. Few people bothered to learn Chinese at Leyden University then. Fewer still could have any hope of ever visiting China, which was accessible only to group tours organized by friends of the Chinese people. These were not my friends. The department of Sinology, housed in a former lunatic asylum, was tiny. My fellow students could be neatly divided into two groups: dreamers enamored by the distant romance of Maoism, and scholars who wanted to spend the rest of their lives grazing such academic fields as Tang poetry or Han dynasty law. I did not fit into either category, and was never a happy Sinologist. I spent more time in that first year dancing with Chinese boys at the DOK disco club in Amsterdam than I did on classical Chinese. The sensual allure of "the East," first glimpsed in those Indian friends in London, was more tangible on the DOK dance floor than in the *Analects* of Confucius.

China seemed impossibly remote, an abstraction really, like a distant planet. And the modern texts we had to read, culled from Communist Party publications like *Red Flag,* or the *People's Daily,* were so deadened by the wooden jargon of official rhetoric, such a sad degradation of the concise beauty of classical Chinese, that my interest in contemporary China soon ran dry. One of the worst insults to the traditional economy of the written Chinese language was the way sentences would run on and on, as though they were literal translations from Karl

Marx's German. And the heavy-handed sarcasm owed more to
the official Soviet style than to anything in the Chinese rhetor-
ical tradition.

Then two things happened to steer me in a different direction. I saw a movie by François Truffaut, entitled *Bed and Board*
(*Domicile Conjugal*). The story was relatively simple. A nice
young man in Paris, named Antoine, played by Truffaut's favorite actor and alter ego Jean-Pierre Léaud, has just got married
to Christine, a nice French girl (Claude Jade). She is already
pregnant with their first child. One day, on a job for an American firm, Antoine meets Kyoko, the daughter of a Japanese
business client: willowy, with long shiny black hair and dark
eyes set in a pale moon face, and dressed in an exquisite kimono,
Kyoko, acted by the famous Pierre Cardin model Hiroko, shim-
mers on the screen like a mysterious Oriental fantasy.

And that is exactly what she turns out to be: a mirage. Antoine is hopelessly smitten by her silky beauty and her strange
and graceful manners: little paper flowers that open in glasses of
water to reveal her amorous sentiments for Antoine, and simi-
larly exotic refinements. Christine, who has had her baby by
now, realizes that Antoine is cheating on her. For a while Antoine
can't help himself, but in the end the dream begins to pall. He
and Kyoko have nothing to say to each other. Paper flowers and
sweet accented nothings are no longer enough. He longs for the
familiar bourgeois certainties of Christine. The Oriental hallu-
cination fades. Antoine comes down to earth. Husband, wife,
and baby son get back together on solid French terrain.

It is a charming film, not Truffaut's very best perhaps, but
wise and funny. I suppose the idea was to warn the viewer not

to be taken in by exotic fantasies; true depth of feeling can only be found with people who have a culture in common. Transcending the borders of language and shared assumptions will result in disillusion.

I'm afraid that I refused to get the message. I fell in love with Kyoko. I wanted a Kyoko in my life, perhaps even more than one. How happy I would be in the land of Kyokos.

More than twenty years later, when I was living in London, I received an invitation to be part of a jury at a modest film festival in France. And there, among my fellow jury members, was a stylish middle-aged Japanese lady dressed in a kimono with a discreet pattern of pink cherry blossoms on a pale blue background. Hiroko, the former Pierre Cardin model and star in Truffaut's film, was now the wife of a grand French fashion executive. I told her how I had once fallen in love with her. She replied in her soft tinkling voice: "*Ça m'arrive souvent*"; you're not the first one to say that.

It must have been around the time I first set eyes on Kyoko, in 1972 or 1973, that I first saw a performance of Terayama Shuji's theater group, Tenjo Sajiki, at the Mickery Theater in Amsterdam. Mickery, located in a former cinema, whose art deco fixtures were left intact, was for some years a mecca of avant-garde theater from all over the world. The young Willem Dafoe performed there with Theatre X and later the Wooster Group. There were groups from Poland, Nigeria, as well as most of the artistic capitals of the West. One of the more memorable visits was by a drama workshop formed by convicts at San Quentin prison in California (young women queued up around the block to meet the ex-cons). I used to go to Mickery regularly, hanging out, as was customary at the time, with the actors in the café after their performances.

Tenjo Sajiki, meaning the cheapest seats in the theater, or "the Gods" in English, was from Tokyo. The founder and director, Terayama Shuji, an aloof but charismatic figure dressed in dark suits and blue high-heeled denim shoes, was a poet, playwright, essayist, novelist, photographer, and filmmaker, who functioned as a kind of Pied Piper in Tokyo, gathering around him a shifting retinue of runaways, misfits, and eccentrics, who acted as living props in his surreal theatrical fantasies. Terayama's plays and movies owed something to various Western influences—a bit of Fellini here, Robert Wilson there—but far more to Japanese fairground entertainments, carnival freaks, striptease shows, and other forms of theatrical lowlife.

Seeing the Tenjo Sajiki for the first time was like squinting through the keyhole of a grotesque peep show full of extraordinary goings-on. I had never seen anything remotely like it. It brought back old memories of magic boxes, lit from the inside, full of strange objects I had concocted with a child's morbid imagination.

The first play I witnessed at the Mickery in 1972 was entitled *Ahen Senso,* or *Opium War.* Less a coherent story than a series of tableaux, *Opium War* was staged outside the theater, as well as inside, where the public was led by a succession of guides into different rooms, decorated with old Japanese movie posters, blown-up details of erotic woodblock prints, lurid comic books, and props that seemed to have been lifted from a 1920s whorehouse. Naked girls were displayed in a variety of peculiar poses, and ventriloquists in chalky Kabuki makeup spoke through dolls dressed like Toulouse-Lautrec while being whipped by a female dominatrix in a black SS cap reciting a Japanese poem. Kimonoed ogres from ancient Japanese ghost stories mingled with men in women's makeup wearing World War II uniforms. One naked man had Chinese characters tattooed all over his body. A beautiful young girl in a purple Chinese dress cut the head off a live chicken. The air of violence and the fact that at certain times we were boxed into metal cages caused an older man in the audience to panic; it reminded him of his incarceration in a Japanese POW camp as a child. During a performance in Germany, members of the audience had accidentally been set on fire. There were rumors of fistfights between actors and the public, which fitted Terayama's vision of theater as a kind of criminal enterprise. All this was accompanied by music, sometimes soft and seductive, sometimes deafening and faintly sinister, a mixture of Pink Floyd–like psychedelic riffs, prewar Japanese popular tunes, and Buddhist chanting, composed and performed by a long-haired man named J. A. Caesar in a top hat. It was deeply weird, over-the-top, largely unintelligible, perversely erotic, rather frightening, and totally unforgettable.

After the performance the petite young actors gathered in the café. But since only a few of them spoke broken English, the barrier between performers and public was barely breached. They were dressed like hip young Westerners—jeans, leather jackets, boots, velvet pants. But some also wore wooden Japanese *geta* and padded kimono jackets. The Tenjo Sajiki seemed to be from a world that was at once familiar, or at least recognizable, and utterly strange. I knew that I had witnessed a theatrical fantasy, but I still thought that if Tokyo was anything like this, I needed to join the circus and get out of town. Going back to the leaden prose of *Red Flag* or the Confucian classics was a letdown after Terayama Shuji and his troupe. To Tokyo, I thought. As soon as possible.

I can't remember what other advice I was given by the man in Amsterdam, apart from staying away from Donald Richie's crowd. Nor did he divulge why Richie's company was so reprehensible. Despite my air of knowingness, I was still a callow youth ("You don't know much about people, do you?" said a Franco-Vietnamese fashion designer, after he picked me up at the DOK disco, where he had bragged about an affair with Alain Delon). But I knew enough to suspect some homosexual rivalry, some fit of social pique. I didn't care: to Tokyo!

The Tenjo Sajiki

TWO

What astonished me about Tokyo on first sight in the fall of
1975 was how much it resembled a Tenjo Sajiki theater
set. I assumed that Terayama's spectacles were the madly exaggerated, surreal fantasies of a poet's feverish mind. To be sure,
I did not come across ventriloquists in nineteenth-century
French clothes being whipped by leather-clad dominatrices. But
there was something theatrical, even hallucinatory, about the
cityscape itself, where nothing was understated; representa-
tions of products, places, entertainment, restaurants, fashion,
and so on were everywhere screaming for attention.

Chinese characters, which I had studied so painstakingly at
Leyden University, loomed high in plastic or neon over freeways
or outside the main railway stations, on banners hanging down
from tall office buildings, on painted signs outside movie theaters and nightclubs known as "cabarets," promising all manner
of diversions that would have been hidden from sight in most
Western cities. In Tokyo, it seemed, very little was out of sight.

Donald Richie, I later learned, did not read Chinese or Japanese script, luckily for him, as his friend the eminent scholar

of Japanese literature Edward Seidensticker once remarked a little tartly: the gracefully painted or luridly neon-lit characters, many of them of very ancient origin, looked beautifully exotic, as long as you didn't know what they signified—commercials for soft drinks, say, or clinics specializing in the treatment of piles (surprisingly common in Japan).

The visual density of Tokyo was overwhelming. In the first few weeks I just walked around in a daze, a lone foreigner bobbing along in crowds of neatly dressed dark-haired people, taking everything in with my eyes, before I learned how to speak properly or read. I just walked and walked, often losing my way in the maze of streets in Shinjuku or Shibuya. Much of the advertising was in the same intense hues as the azure skies of early autumn. I realized now that the colors in old Japanese woodcuts were not stylized at all, but an accurate depiction of Japanese light. Plastic chrysanthemums in burnt orange and gold were strung along the narrow shopping streets to mark the season. The visual barrage of neon lights, crimson lanterns, and movie posters was matched by the cacophony of mechanical noise: from Japanese pop tunes, advertising jingles, record stores, cabarets, theaters, and PA systems in train stations, and blaring forth from TV sets left on all day and night in coffee shops, bars, and restaurants. It made J. A. Caesar's background music to the Tenjo Sajiki plays seem almost hushed.

I did not delve into the thick of Japanese life immediately. For several weeks, before looking for an apartment with my girlfriend, Sumie, I stayed in a kind of buffer zone, a cultural halfway house. A British relative, named Ashley Raeburn, was the representative of Shell in Japan. He lived with his wife, Nest, in a huge mansion in Aobadai, a plush hilly district high above the tumult of the main commercial hubs of the city. Behind the house was a wide sloping lawn, kept green in all seasons, where we played croquet on Sundays. The sound of sprinklers reminded me of my childhood in The Hague. Ashley was driven to his work in a Rolls-Royce. Food was served at a long chestnut table, polished to a high sheen, by one of the uniformed staff, summoned after each course with a bell. The contrast with the city I took in with my eyes and ears during the day could not have been greater. As long as I stayed with Ashley and Nest, Tokyo was still a spectacle, a kind of theater, from which I could retreat every evening into the quasi-colonial opulence of Aobadai.

The only glimpses I got of a strictly Japanese world in Ashley's mansion were entirely belowstairs, as they used to call it in grand English country houses. Sitting by the fire with Ashley and Nest, cradling an after-dinner whiskey while discussing Japan and the Japanese, was comfortable enough. But I preferred having endless cups of green tea in the kitchen, trying hard to straighten out my broken Japanese with the chauffeur, a jokey ex-policeman, or the cook, and the kind ladies who served us at dinner. Being given rides in the Shell Rolls-Royce made me feel conspicuous and was something of an embarrassment. But my preference for belowstairs was less a matter of reverse snobbery than a desire to penetrate the mysteries of Japan. If I was to fit in, I had better learn fast. It was in the kitchen that I received my first lessons in linguistic etiquette, how to use different forms depending on who I was talking to. The chauffeur and the cook could address me in familiar language, since I was much younger than they were. But I had to address them in more deferential terms. Not just idioms, but personal pronouns and even verb endings change according to age, gender, and social status. This essential part of the Japanese language is not only hard to master at first, but becomes increasingly important as one's skill improves. One difficulty I faced was that I spoke feminine Japanese by mimicking my girlfriend, which made me sound a bit like a simpering drag queen. And I would soon learn that the more fluent one became in Japanese, the more jarring slips in etiquette would sound to the native ear. Since my Japanese was still quite basic, my infelicities at Aobadai were forgiven.

Roaming around Tokyo by day, I thought of my culture shock when I first saw Los Angeles, that sense of being on a huge movie set, quickly built and quick to come down, with its architectural fantasies of Tudor, Mexican Moorish, Scottish Baronial, and French beaux arts. It was a shock because I had never seen such a city before. Accustomed to the solidity of historic cities in Europe, I was both fascinated by LA and a trifle smug, as though growing up in a more antique environment conveyed some kind of moral superiority. Tokyo, like many postwar Asian cities, with their ubiquitous billboards and strip malls, owed a lot to the Southern Californian model, but Tokyo's density—the crowds, the noise, the visual excess—made LA seem staid in comparison.

One particular coffee shop sticks in my mind as a typical example of the city I first saw in the mid-1970s. It was called

Versailles, located underground, near the east exit of Shinjuku station, one of the largest stations in Tokyo. To get there you had to go down some steep concrete steps, with the noise of advertising jingles from a famous camera store still ringing in your ears. All of a sudden, there you were, in the drawing room of an eighteenth-century French château, with candelabras, marble walls, gilded Louis XIV–ish furniture, and the sound of baroque music. Naturally, everything was made of plastic and plywood. People spent hours in this ersatz splendor, smoking and reading comic books, while listening to Richard Clayderman tinkling *Eine kleine Nachtmusik*. Versailles was demolished a long time ago, as were most coffee shops of that time. There might be a Starbucks there now, or a restaurant offering a fusion of Japanese and northern Italian cuisine.

Much of what I first observed in 1975 had been built in the 1960s, when the economic boom was gathering speed. Nothing much older was to be seen, apart from some temples and shrines, and a few early twentieth century brick buildings that survived firestorms and bombs. Tokyo had been modernized along Western lines in the late nineteenth century, half destroyed by an earthquake in 1923, and reduced to miles of rubble by American bombs in 1945. The sixties were a great period for cheap fantasy architecture. After years of austerity following the ruinous war, there was a hunger for real, but mostly still imaginary, luxury. Few Japanese in those days had the means to travel abroad, and so a make-believe abroad was built in Japan to cater to people's dreams, hence the Louis XIV cafés, or the German beer halls, or a well-known short-time hotel, named the Queen Elizabeth 2, built of concrete in the shape of an ocean liner, complete with recorded foghorns.

The first Disneyland to be built outside the United States was in Japan, in 1983, not far from Narita International Airport. Donald Richie once wrote that there was no need for one, for the Japanese already had a Disneyland called Tokyo. The nonresidential areas of the city certainly had the ephemeral air of a theme park. Richie's admirer, Christopher Isherwood, the British novelist who had made Los Angeles his home after living in Berlin before the war, wrote the following words about his adopted city: "What was there, on this shore, a hundred years ago? And which, of all these flimsy structures, will be standing a hundred years from now? Probably not a single one. Well, I like that thought. It is bracingly realistic. In such surroundings, it is easier to remember and accept the fact that you won't be here, either."*

There is something very Japanese in this sentiment, the quiet acceptance of evanescence. I quoted Isherwood's words at the memorial for Norman Yonemoto, who died in Los Angeles in 2014.

I think Isherwood would have liked Tokyo in the 1970s. The wartime gloom had made way for frenetic hedonism. But above all, the sense of illusion would have appealed to his penchant for Oriental mysticism, the idea of the fleetingness of things. There is nevertheless an important difference between Tokyo and LA. History does not run deep in LA, whereas Tokyo, or Edo as it used to be called, was already a small castle town in the twelfth

---

* *Exhumations,* London: Methuen, 1966.

century. In the eighteenth century, Edo was the second-largest city in the world, after Beijing. So the plastic-fantastic Tokyo I encountered in 1975, with its motley collection of pastiche buildings, owing something to many parts of the world, albeit in a much altered form, was built on deep layers of history.

The palimpsest that is modern Tokyo still shows traces of its past, in the layout of the streets, for example. But history mostly lives on in historical memory expressed in popular culture, as myth. Even the very recent past was steeped in legend in Tokyo. Just a few years into the new decade, the sixties were already remembered in a haze of nostalgia for youthful rebellion and experiment. "You should have been here then," the old hands would say. Ah, the student demos in 1968, the underground theater performances at Hanazono Shrine, the "happenings" near Shinjuku station, where the local hippies known as *futenzoku* (crazy tribe) hung out, the early movies of Oshima Nagisa, the posters by Yokoo Tadanori, Shinoyama Kishin's photography, the foundation of Butoh dance by Hijikata Tatsumi.

By the time I arrived, the *futenzoku* had moved on. You were more likely to encounter the last mutilated World War II veterans in white kimonos and wooden limbs playing sad wartime ballads on accordions at Shinjuku station than hippies strumming guitars. Some would say that the party came to a neatly timed end in 1970 with the suicide of Mishima Yukio, the novelist who staged his violent samurai death by slitting his stomach surrounded by his uniformed band of handsome young militiamen after a failed coup d'état at a military base in the middle of Tokyo. In fact, cultures don't end so much as mutate. By 1975, the rebels of the previous decades, including Terayama Shuji, had become respected figures, were given prestigious prizes, and were invited to international festivals.

Perhaps it is the speed of destruction and construction in Tokyo that evokes nostalgia. There was always a "then" that was sorely missed. Not so very long ago the entire city was made up of canals and wooden houses, which regularly went up in flames in firestorms called the "Flowers of Edo." Very few buildings were meant to last forever: no great stone cathedrals. The monumental is not part of the Japanese style. History in Tokyo is only visible in fragments: a ruined nobleman's garden here, a rebuilt Shinto shrine there, or a tiny bar, now sadly forsaken, where Mishima once held court.

Donald Richie was a young reporter for the *Stars and Stripes* army newspaper when he wandered around the streets of Asakusa in 1947, just two years after they had been flattened in American bombing raids. Flanking the Sumida River in the plebeian east end of Tokyo, Asakusa had been the liveliest popular entertainment district in the city for about a hundred years, filled with movie houses, burlesque theaters, cafés and bars, brothels and dance halls, street markets and temple fairs. Asakusa was the setting of Kawabata Yasunari's earliest stories about gangsters and showgirls in the Roaring Twenties. This was the widely lamented period of *ero, guro, nansensu*—erotic, grotesque, absurd.

Richie climbed the old Subway Tower building in Asakusa together with Kawabata, who was dressed in a simple winter kimono. Neither could speak a word of the other's language. All they could do was point at the shabby knocked-together landscape of early postwar Tokyo. Richie would mention the name of a character in one of Kawabata's early stories and the writer would smile wanly and point to a place where he imagined them to have lived. The destruction of his city did not seem to have fazed Kawabata; it was still there in his imagination.

In the 1960s, one of Terayama Shuji's favorite experiments was to perform his theatrical spectacles in the streets. *Throw Away Your Books, Rally in the Streets* was the title of one of his most famous plays. He wanted to break down the barriers between artistic performance and the performance of daily life. His actors, kitted out in costumes from different periods—1920s vamps, nineteenth-century dandies, 1960s *futenzoku*—mingled with the crowds, shocking people out of their normal routines. The Tenjo Sajiki was not the only theater troupe in those days to try to infuse real life with fantasy. The difference with similar experiments in Paris, or New York, or Amsterdam, was that in Tokyo there was less of a barrier between fantasy and reality to break down.

THERE WAS NOTHING EXOTIC about Nihon University College of Art, or Nichidai for short, where I was supposed to be studying cinema. The buildings, probably erected in the late 1950s or early 1960s, were so nondescript that I cannot remember exactly what they looked like. Ekoda, where the campus was located, was a sprawling suburb of wood and stucco houses, with a narrow shopping street festooned with plastic flowers winding its way to the station on the Seibu Ikebukuro line.

In fact, I never studied cinema at Nichidai very seriously. The professors were mostly cordial men who had never made a film in their lives, but had stayed on to teach after they graduated from the school themselves. The dean was a fussy bureaucrat who spoke and dressed like the branch manager of a middling bank. His connection to the movies, if any, was tenuous.

But one professor did leave a lasting impression. His name was Ushihara Kiyohiko, a tiny gentleman with a wet toothy grin who must have been in his early eighties. He spoke a great deal about Charlie Chaplin, his idol, whom he had assisted in Hollywood for a time in the 1920s. He called him *"Chapurin-sensei."* More than once the old man acted out the Tramp in front of the class, taking mincing little steps and twirling an imaginary cane, while explaining camera angles. After he returned to Japan from Hollywood in 1927, Ushihara went on to specialize in tearjerkers (known in Japan as "three-handkerchief films"), soaked in nostalgia for bygone eras when life was more traditional, simpler, warmer. *Love of Life* was one of his successes, which earned him the nickname Sentimental Ushihara. He later made a few films in another genre called *supotsu mono,* or sports films, about baseball heroes and the like—Japanese movie genres used to be like Tokyo coffee shops that catered to jazz lovers, classical music buffs, or rock fans, carefully categorized in terms of taste.

Most of my knowledge of Sentimental Ushihara comes from Donald Richie's books. His movies are hard to track down. I did manage to see a fascinating early work heavily influenced by French impressionism, which he had not actually directed but had written the script for, called *Souls on the Road* (1921).

This silent movie about a failed violinist, inspired by Gorky's *The Lower Depths,* was remarkable for being the first Japanese film to use female actors instead of men impersonating women in the Kabuki style.

I failed to get the full benefit of Ushihara's classes, alas. Even the Chaplin anecdotes, told and retold with unflagging enthusiasm, were only partly intelligible to me, not just because he slushed his words with a great deal of froth, but because my Japanese was not yet good enough to understand what the old man was saying.

The student films I saw were equally hard to follow, but mostly because of the use of slang. One of the stars on campus, whose name I can't recall, was often seen slouching about, always with an entourage of young men, all dressed in black leather jackets and sunglasses, worn day and night. Most of his short films revolved around slouching young men in black leather jackets and sunglasses, who died in scenes of spectacular violence. Women in these student films spent most of the time being abused in one way or another. This invariably involved taking their clothes off. Intrigued, I asked fellow students about these amateur actresses. They assured me that Japanese girls would do this at the drop of a hat for me, because they were like putty in the hands of a foreigner, or *gaijin*. This was an entrenched and pretty much universal belief in Japan in those days, perhaps going back to the time when Japan was occupied by American troops.

To be sure, the gaijin status had its perks. One reminder of the turbulent 1960s on the Ekoda campus was the library of English-language books, which, curiously for an educational institution, was off limits to the students. The reason, I was told, was that students had occupied the library during one of the big protest demonstrations in 1968, or perhaps 1970. Japanese students were fiercely opposed to the Vietnam War and their own government's complicity in it. Since then, only foreign students were allowed to go into the stacks. As there were only, so far as I could tell, two other foreign students at the art school, the library was effectively vacant.

A large gangly administrator unlocked the library door for me. He had just returned from a vacation in America, and was dressed in full Western gear: boots, a garishly checked Western shirt with silver buttons, and a bolo tie. The library had the musty smell of a place that needed a proper airing. There was one other person there, picking up various books from the shelves. He was clearly one of the two other foreign students. I had met one already, an American named Rich, who insisted on addressing me in Japanese, even when I answered him pointedly in English. I tended to dodge him on campus. The one perusing the stacks, wearing a blue cotton Japanese kimono jacket, was still a stranger to me. His name was Graham, an Englishman. Graham was studying the Noh theater—when he wasn't staging "performances" in Harajuku, dancing along the main thoroughfare in a long white dress with a poet called Shiraishi Kazuko, who enjoyed a scandalous reputation (she was rumored to have slept with Muhammad Ali). She, too, had made her reputation in the 1960s.

It soon became evident that almost every book in the English-language section of the library had been the property of one man. His name was scribbled on the title pages of most of the books: Cecil Postlethwaite (or something like that). Next to his name was the date and place of residence: Berlin 1929, Berlin 1930, all the way to Berlin 1936, when perhaps things were becoming a little too hot even for Postlethwaite, and the dateline changed to Tokyo 1937, Tokyo 1938, and so on. I don't know what happened to him during the war. Presumably he was interned as an enemy alien. Or he might have died before Pearl Harbor.

Postlethwaite's literary taste was as specialized in its way as Ushihara's tearjerkers: several rare first editions of Oscar Wilde's plays, as well as signed memoirs by long-forgotten society ladies who had known the great playwright; the complete works of Ronald Firbank; books on Greek sculpture; a slim volume, published in Dresden, about nudists in Germany, richly illustrated with photographs of athletic young men bathing. Quite how this collection ended up at the Nichidai library in Ekoda is a mystery. I cannot imagine there would have been much call for these books, even if students had been allowed in. But the slightly stale whiff of prewar pederasty lingering in this dreary suburb of Tokyo appealed to the imagination of Graham and myself. We later rather regretted that we had not pocketed some of the rarer items, before repairing to the classical music coffee shop opposite Ekoda station called Zigeunerweisen.

Postlethwaite was one of those readers who liked to express his feelings in the margins: exclamation marks of agreement, question marks denoting skepticism, and comments, like "rubbish!" or "quite so!" I randomly picked up a book of short stories by Somerset Maugham. One of them was about a British planter in a remote area of Malaya. An old friend from home has come to pay him a visit. They are having gin and tonics on the veranda at sundown. The friend asks him how he can bear to live in such an isolated spot, where one would almost never meet a fellow white man. The planter replies that this is precisely why he chose to live there. This sentence was underlined in the book with almost ferocious stress by its owner.

It was not hard to imagine a man like Postlethwaite, an escapee from middle-class England, a sexual exile first in Germany, and later in Japan. There were others like him. Christopher Isherwood had moved to Berlin for similar reasons. Tropical and subtropical places, from Capri to Ceylon, especially in days of empire, were dotted with private Arcadias built by such men who refused to live in puritanical Anglo-Saxon countries where their sexual desires could land them in prison. They often resided in lovely traditional houses in secluded spots, filled with fine furniture and art, with handsome and willing young men to lend a hand when needed.

One of the first people I met in Japan was a figure rather like this, another acquaintance of my gay uncle. John Roderick was a veteran American reporter who had spent part of the war with Mao Zedong's Communist guerrillas in the caves of Yan'an. After the war, when Western journalists were no longer welcome in China, he based himself in Japan. Roderick was not a handsome man. He looked like a retired sergeant major, burly, with a large jaw, a clipped moustache, and small watery blue eyes peering amiably from a large florid face. His Japanese was rudimentary, but he was not shy, and never short of company.

Roderick lived on a hill overlooking Kamakura, the graceful

old capital of medieval Japan, one of the few towns to have escaped the wartime bombings, filled with Buddhist temples and
Shinto shrines. On top of that hill, he had built his Arcadia: a
gorgeous old farmhouse with a thatched roof, dark brown timber floors, ocher mud walls, rice paper sliding doors, eighteenth-
century lacquered screens, gilded wooden sculptures of Buddhist
deities, precious Edo Period tea bowls, and finely crafted antique
chests. The farmhouse had been dismantled in a village in central Japan and rebuilt, timber for timber, by traditional Japanese
carpenters. This entire enterprise had been arranged by a young
man of extraordinary beauty whom Roderick had spotted some
years before at a public swimming pool. They had lived together
ever since. Yoshihiro, or Yo-chan, as he was affectionately
called, was officially adopted as Roderick's son.

It was through John Roderick that I met Donald Richie, a
few months after I arrived. We were both invited for dinner,
specifically for this purpose, at the Tokyo apartment of another
middle-aged expatriate, an English writer and traveler named
John Haylock. He, too, was a sexual refugee, who had lived in
a succession of congenial tropical homes, in Baghdad, Cyprus,
Thailand, and now Japan, where he taught English literature
at a girls' college. Haylock wrote in his memoir, entitled *Eastern Exchange:* "I felt it was wiser to live in a tolerant land . . .
It was better to be in self-exile than a potential criminal."

John was not very old, in his early sixties at most. I asked
him, perhaps a little gauchely, how long he intended to live in
Japan. Well, he replied, "I believe I shall die here, which I rather
think might be very soon." Talking to John was like shaking
hands, metaphorically at least, with the Bloomsbury group; he

had been on intimate terms with Duncan Grant and had known Violet Trefusis, Virginia Woolf's lover, in Paris. He also knew Mishima, as did most of Donald's friends. To be able to say "I knew Mishima" was a badge of honor, cherished by literary-minded veterans of the Tokyo gay scene.

So this then was "Donald Richie's crowd," about which the man in Amsterdam had warned me. I felt instantly at ease with them, even though I was hardly a sexual exile myself. My own yearnings were more for the Kyoko I had seen in Truffaut's film than for a Yo-chan, although I could very well see the attractions of both. Like many young men, I was in a hurry to make up for lost adolescent opportunities, and hungry for experience. But I was hedging my bets, for I still had a safe haven, a home that minimized my risk.

This temporary home was a six-tatami-mat room and a four-and-a-half-mat bedroom in a rickety apartment building on the Seibu Shinjuku railway line, which I shared with my girlfriend, Sumie, who had returned to Japan just before I arrived. I was glad to leave the luxurious seclusion of my relative's house, where I had spent the first weeks in Japan. We found the apartment after doing the rounds of real estate agents, most of whom were too polite to turn a foreigner down outright. But we had to understand that landlords might be worried that the gaijin-san didn't know the proper way of using a Japanese bathroom, or might give the neighbors a fright, or would abscond without paying. Why, only the other day, there was such a case with an American. . . .

Sumie did not really fit in either. Having escaped from the

strictures of her childhood home in a provincial Japanese town, she had been in no hurry to come back. Like many young Japanese women who sought a degree of independence that was not generally on offer at home, she preferred to live abroad. Having decided that she wanted to be in a small country, she had picked Holland more or less at random on the map, gathered up all her savings, and traveled alone by boat and train via the Siberian plains to Europe. She was a tougher person than I was. We had met in a Chinese restaurant in Leyden, where we were both studying and she was working part time to pay the rent.

For a year and a half, Sumie and I shared that apartment in Numabukuro. The elusive Kyokos remained figments of my imagination. We were happy together. But I also felt I was missing out on something. I wasn't ready to settle down, but I yearned for security too. It was easier to live dangerously in a vicarious way, like peering into the opium-scented brothels in Terayama's plays, or rubbing shoulders with Donald Richie's crowd, which had some of the glamour of my uncle's set in London. Knowingness still came more easily to me than the potential sting of experience. Life still felt more like a performance.

Perhaps it was because of my childhood in a culturally mixed household, or possibly something else in my makeup, that I always felt drawn to outsiders. But outsiders, including Donald Richie's friends, form their own exclusive groups. I could pass, but I would not commit. Hovering on the fringes was where I liked to be, neither in nor out, neither one thing nor another, semidetached, a born fellow traveler, a male fag hag, an observer in the midst of sympathetic strangers. It was thrilling, but also a way of playing it safe. Perhaps that was why I was attracted to Japan, a society to which a foreigner could never belong, even if he wanted to.

Donald was dressed like a conventional middle-class American: light blue jacket, gray shirt, a knitted maroon tie, big black Florsheim shoes. He looked young for his age, which would have been around fifty-three: pink cheeks, brownish hair, large white hands, a boyish midwestern face that slightly resembled that of Alfred Kinsey, the famous sexologist. The range of his conversation was astonishing: Japanese movie world gossip, Arnold Schoenberg's expressionist songs, Ozu Yasujiro's films compared to Kurosawa Akira's, Jane Austen's late novels. But his main subject, especially when he was addressing me as the newcomer, was the way foreigners lived in Japan.

He pointed out the pitfalls that many gaijin stumbled into: namely the speed with which infatuation could change into disenchantment, or even peevish resentment, as though Japan were to blame for personal disillusion. He mentioned the "Seidensticker syndrome," named after his friend, the scholar Edward Seidensticker. Ed habitually spent half the year in Japan. When he arrived in Tokyo, he was ready to kiss the ground. Everything was wonderful. Then, once he had more or less settled down, he began to get more and more irritated by "these people," until after six months he was quite ready to go home.

The great mistake, Donald told me, was to think that you could ever be treated in the same way as a Japanese. People would be polite, even warm. Profound friendships with Japanese were perfectly possible. But you would never be one of them. You would always be an "outside person," the literal meaning of "gaijin."

Donald Richie

Those foreigners who were foolish enough to resent this could easily develop a full-blown case of gaijinitis, in which every sign of special treatment, whether deferential or contemptuous, was seen as a bitter blow to their amour propre.

He, Donald, felt entirely at ease as an outsider. The great thing about Japan, he said, was that one was left alone. To be Japanese in Japan was to be caught in an almost intolerable web of rules and obligations. But the gaijin was exempt from all that. He could observe life with serene detachment, not being bound to anything or anyone. In Japan, Donald felt utterly, radically free.

For a man of Donald's inclinations this would clearly have been impossible in Lima, Ohio, where he grew up dreaming of escape. But even in New York, where he lived in the late 1960s as the curator of film at the Museum of Modern Art, he still felt constrained. So he came back to Japan just a few years before I met him, not exactly as a sexual exile, but as a man who was convinced that when he first arrived in Japan in the late 1940s he had glimpsed his private Arcadia: a country where he would never be judged for his desires.

"You know," he said, before we parted company at the Hongo subway station, "you have to be a romantic to live in Japan. A person who feels complete, who does not question who he is, or his place in the world, will dislike it here. To be constantly exposed to such a radically different culture becomes unbearable. But to a romantic, open to other ways of being, Japan is full of wonders. Not that you will ever belong here. But that will set you free. And freedom is better than belonging. You see, here you can make yourself into anything you want to be."

I'm not sure I knew exactly what he meant by this. Much later, he would explain his allegiance to Sartre's existential views on the need to create your own life as an act of will to be authentic. But the image of Donald that night, standing on the opposite station platform, with his pink cheeks and big black shoes, unassailable in the midst of crowds of Japanese, has stayed with me. Perhaps I felt liberated too. What to make of myself was the question.

THREE

never thought I could be Japanese, nor did I wish to be. But I suppose I was a romantic in Richie's sense of the word. I was open to change. This meant, in the early stages of my life in Japan, almost total immersion. The fact that I was living with a Japanese woman in a middle-class suburb on the Seibu Shinjuku commuter line, surrounded by noodle shops, Shinto shrines, public bathhouses, and old wooden houses with bonsai gardens helped.

You could still hear some of the traditional sounds of urban Japanese life then: the plaintive cry, a bit like a muezzin calling Muslims to prayer, of the sweet potato vendors, the dry crack of wooden clappers struck at night by the neighborhood fire watchmen, the foghorn sounds of the tofu sellers, the haunting drone of a bronze bell from a local temple. Less traditional were the jingles and recorded messages from political candidates, waving their white-gloved hands from passing cars, even if the streets were empty, and there was no one to wave back. Then there were the scurrying feet of the "family health" merchants after they had deposited a basket filled with condoms at the door, to be returned if not required.

Visiting Sumie's family home in Gifu, a provincial town about 160 miles to the west of Tokyo, meant an even deeper immersion into traditional Japanese life. Tani-san, her father, a war veteran who had served in the Imperial Japanese Army in China, was a sign painter. As a member of the artisan class, he took pride in his independence and his artistic skill. His way of life was more old-fashioned and relaxed than that of most so-called salarymen, the white-collar army of gray-suited straphangers commuting every day to their offices from tiny apartments in the outer suburbs. More often than not, salarymen in the 1970s had left the traditional duties of communal living with extended families behind. The modern nuclear family was seen as a kind of liberation, even if it resulted in lonely isolation, especially for the wives waiting up at night for their husbands to stagger home from social functions imposed on the lower-ranking office workers.

Independent craftsmen were different. Three generations of Tanis lived in a cozy two-story wooden house in an old part of town, smelling of fresh tatami mats, incense from the local temple, and dodgy drains. Japan is now famous for its luxurious toilets, with electric heated seats, automatic flush, different varieties of spray, and tinkling music. But in his masterful essay, *In Praise of Shadows,* the novelist Tanizaki Junichiro extolled the virtues of the traditional "dimly lit" wooden Japanese toilet, where one contemplated the beauties of nature while squatting over a hole in the ground with boughs of cedar at the bottom to sweeten the smell. Such toilets barely exist anymore. The Tanis still had one, even though the beauties of nature were not in sight. "Night soil" collectors would come to the house every so often to pick up the waste to fertilize the fields outside town.

The family also shared a communal bathtub of fragrant hinoki wood. Seniority dictated the order of bathing. As soap was used only outside the tub, the water remained relatively clean, even for the last one to use it. If one happened upon a person emerging from the bathroom without any clothes on, Grandmother, say, one pretended not to have seen her. Sometimes, for sheer pleasure, we would go to the local public bathhouse, the *sento,* with its tiled walls decorated with vistas of Mount Fuji, where we gossiped with the neighbors while politely splashing one another's backs from small bamboo buckets.

I don't wish to idealize the life of the Tanis. Their extended family was as prone to bitter rows and irreconcilable feuds as any other. And the way the family was bossed around by the authoritarian grandfather, a former railway official, before he died not long after my arrival, made the decision of salarymen's wives to plump for splendid isolation in high-rise apartments more understandable. But there was a generosity of spirit in the Tani household, a broad-mindedness that was often lacking in more prosperous families, where social face had to be more carefully guarded.

One generational clash that would later explode in permanent estrangement between father and eldest son concerned the different attitudes toward their advertising business. The son, named Kazuo, regarded his father's artisanal pride in hand-painted shop signs or movie billboards, carefully copied from film stills, as so much waste of time. He preferred to use plastic models, or other technological shortcuts, which he regarded, not without reason, as cheaper and more with the times. He saw himself not as a craftsman but as a modern businessman.

But this rift had not yet erupted when I first stayed with the Tanis. The workshop was built as an extension of the main family room, where the television was permanently switched on, and we ate our meals. The parents and grandmother slept there too, in bedding rolled out on the tatami floor at night. The rest of us slept on the first floor near the Buddhist altar, where Grandmother prayed every morning to the black-and-white photograph of her late husband placed in the midst of offerings of fruit and rice cakes. The workshop was filled with cans of paint, slabs of hardboard, and movie posters. Since the main commercial fare in the mid-1970s consisted of a heavy diet of soft-porn films, produced by the Nikkatsu movie studio, the family took its simple dinners of fish, rice, and miso soup surrounded by lurid images of helpless young housewives trussed up in ropes by gangsters in leather jackets and sunglasses.

After dinner, before I had my bath, Kazuo would often take me to the local Nikkatsu movie theater, where he enjoyed free access, to see some of these films. They were much more interesting than the student movies I had seen, which were clearly modeled after them. Indeed, they were more interesting than any porn film I had ever seen in the West, which were mostly coarse, leering, and unimaginative.

A discussion of seventies culture in Japan would be incomplete without reference to *roman porno,* or porno romance, the official name of this specific genre, which attracted some of the most talented young directors. Forget about Ozu and Kurosawa, I was frequently told by fellow students at the Nichidai film school, go and see Kumashiro Tatsumi's movies, featuring Ichijo Sayuri, the most popular *roman porno* star at the time. Ichijo had had a distinguished career as a stripper in Osaka. Many of the pictures she starred in had inventive plots and were technically accomplished, even innovative. This was not just because it was getting harder for young talent to break into the fast crumbling studio system. Porno was now the favored genre of leftists who were disillusioned by the failure of political activism in the sixties. Japan had effectively been a one-party state for several decades, ruled by the conservative Liberal Democrats, overseen by an entrenched bureaucracy, and manipulated by industrial combines, agricultural lobbies, and American security interests. After more than ten years of student protest, the militant left had come apart in ultraviolent factions like the Japanese Red Army, exploding in spectacular and often suicidal acts of terrorism. Red Army fighters ended up dead, or in places like Pyongyang and Beirut, while some of their cinematic fellow travelers drifted into porno. Thwarted political subversion had morphed into socioerotic rebellion. This resulted in at least one genuine masterpiece.

Oshima Nagisa released his hard-core sex film, *In the Realm of the Senses,* in 1976. His earlier movies had been highly political: about discrimination against Koreans, student activism, crime as a form of social protest, or oppression in the slums of Osaka. Now he would see how far he could push freedom of expression by making a pornographic art film. *In the Realm of the Senses* was a huge *succès de scandale*, based on a true story, set in the 1920s. The film depicted a passionate love affair between a former prostitute, named Abe Sada, and a restaurant owner, named Kichizo, which ended in his violent death after a bout of rough sex. The rough sex included Sada's attempts to heighten her lover's ecstasy by almost strangling him with the sash of her kimono, a game that became less and less playful as time went on, until it proved to be fatal. In a fit of madness, Sada cut off the main object of her desire, including the testicles, and stuffed it into her purse.

No filmmaker had ever pulled off anything like this before. The movie was both hard core and tender, a cinematic blow for sexual freedom, especially for women. Sada, the prostitute, played by Matsuda Eiko, a former actress in Terayama Shuji's Tenjo Sajiki, is not a helpless object of male lust but an equal partner in an erotic obsession (which did not prevent Matsuda's career from sinking into oblivion, even opprobrium, while her male counterpart, Fuji Tatsuya, became a star).*

After the film was first shown at the Cannes Film Festival, I went to see Terayama Shuji at the Tenjo Sajiki headquarters in Shibuya, a fizzy area in the west of Tokyo, where he lived in a small apartment, allegedly with his mother—the theatrical wizard's own sexuality was a bit of a mystery; he had a history of being reprimanded by the local police for peeping into people's bedrooms. Terayama had seen Oshima's movie at Cannes. His mouth tightened when I asked him about it: "Not very interesting at all," he said. "Most *roman porno* films are much better." I suspected that envy had affected his usually sound judgment.

---

* The real Abe Sada was finally arrested in Tokyo. After spending some years in prison, she opened a bar in Asakusa, where, according to Donald Richie, who was often there, she would make a grand entrance at the same time every night, eagerly anticipated by the male patrons, who would all cup their genitals in unison. Abe spent the last years of her life in a nunnery.

Oshima's movie provoked a notorious obscenity trial in Japan—not against the film itself, which couldn't be released in its original form, but against the publication of the script illustrated by photographic stills. Oshima's wonderful defense was: "So what's wrong with obscenity?" He was acquitted.

Alas, most Japanese never had the chance to judge for themselves. By the time the movie came to Tokyo, the print had been so badly mutilated by the censors, who were obliged to eliminate every sign of human genitals with razor blades and Vaseline, that Oshima's masterpiece was unwatchable. Quite why people were not allowed to see genitals on the screen, even though mixed bathing in public hot springs was still relatively common in rural areas, is a bit of a mystery. Probably this had something to do with a tug-of-war that went back centuries between the authorities, insisting on public order and social control, and unruly artists, insisting on subverting it.

Certainly puritanism, of the Christian kind, is not a part of Japanese tradition. Kazuo had no doubt that taking me to the porno theater after dinner was a fitting entertainment. There was no shame attached to it, any more than that anyone felt embarrassed about sharing a family bath. But again, Sumie's was an old-fashioned household. Perhaps censorious attitudes were more prevalent among the higher, more Westernized classes.

I believe this is what Donald Richie was getting at when he stressed what he called the "innocence" of the Japanese. "The Japanese" was still a phrase that was used readily by men of Richie's generation. Soon after meeting him for dinner with John Roderick, Donald became my mentor on things concerning "the Japanese." He was the sensei. I would be his disciple, or *deshi*. We had regular lunches near a publisher's office in Roppongi, where he did editing work in the afternoons, and talked about the Japanese.

By innocence I think Donald meant the lack of any consciousness of original sin, in the Christian sense. Sexual behavior was kept in check by propriety, not by religious proscriptions, or threats of metaphysical doom. And propriety was something that concerned the guardians of social order, hence their reaction to Oshima's film. *Roman porno,* whose clever directors found ever more ingenious ways to avoid the censor's razor blades, was far less radical than Oshima's film, but breathed the same imaginative spirit of freedom.

Since the privileged gaijin was exempted from many Japanese proprieties, Japan in the 1940s must have seemed like

Fuji Tatsuya on the set of Oshima Nagisa's movie
Empire of Passion (1978)

paradise to a young American raised in small-town Ohio. Donald never built a private Arcadia in the way others, like John Roderick, had done: no beautiful old house filled with antique screens. He did, for a while, live in such a house, belonging to another sexual exile, an American art book publisher named Meredith "Tex" Weatherby, whose late boyfriend had taken a famous photograph of Mishima posing in nothing but a loincloth in the snow-covered garden and brandishing a samurai sword. There were many stories of wild times back in the day. I only remember Tex in his later years, a large shambling man peering over his bifocals while he was doing needlepoint.

Despite living in Weatherby's house for some time, Donald did not much like the company of gay men. John Roderick irritated him with his habit of calling men "she" and pretending that everyone from George Washington to John Wayne was a screaming queen.

Donald's Arcadia was his ideal of innocence. One of his prize possessions, which he kept with him wherever he lived, and would show proudly to his friends, was a collection of photo albums, neatly lined up on his bookshelves, that contained, like so many pinned-up butterflies, photographs of his sexual conquests, going back to the late 1940s. They were of a type, these wide-eyed, handsome country boys, grinning in some steaming hot spring bath, relaxing on the tatami floor of a country inn, playfully flexing muscles in a white T-shirt, or leaning against a truck. Nobuo was a bus driver, Shinichi a builder, Yasuo a baseball coach, and so on. They were all straight. Or so Donald liked to believe.

. . .

MY OWN JAPANESE IMMERSION did not involve a quest for innocence. I did not grow up in Ohio, haunted by original sin. The
pleasure I took in hearing of Donald's escapades was vicarious.
Instead, I was knocking on the doors of prominent figures in
theater and film, which often sprang open with surprising ease.
Famous directors would come and meet me for coffee, even
though they probably had a hard time understanding my faulty
Japanese. I still wince a little at the thought of Suzuki Tadashi,
one of the grandest people in the modern Japanese theater,
patiently hearing me gush on about performances I had seen of
his group, the Waseda Shogekijo, at the Mickery Theater in
Amsterdam, and listening to my callow questions about the
influence of the Kabuki on contemporary drama. Suzuki, the
son of a Noh actor, was an intellectual. He answered in rapid
sentences that I could barely follow.

Being able to meet such grandees at short notice was part
of the gaijin's privilege. There were so few Westerners in Tokyo
at that time with an interest in modern Japanese drama or film,
that one had the advantage of rarity. People like me piqued the
curiosity of people who otherwise wouldn't have given us the
time of day. Donald Richie was a pioneer in this field; indeed,
he had played an important role himself in the Tokyo culture
of the sixties, when he made a number of experimental films
with music scores by the great Takemitsu Toru. But in this he
was pretty much alone.

Years later—sometime in the 1980s—I was at a screening
in Tokyo of Donald's short films. The event was organized for

the benefit of his friend the American poet James Merrill. Next to me sat Edward Seidensticker, looking professorial in jacket and tie. He had brought a family friend from the States, a very proper-looking young lady in a beige woolen twinset. One of the films was entitled *Boy with Cat*. A handsome young Japanese boy in white jeans is seen in the moody shadows of a traditional Japanese room with summer noises in the background: the rasp of cicadas, a child practicing Beethoven's *Moonlight Sonata*. While the boy is leafing through a set of (heterosexual) pornographic pictures, he sticks his hand into his jeans and masturbates. A black cat jumps onto his thigh. The music abruptly stops, signaling the end of the movie. When the lights went on, there was a moment of silence in the screening room. Professor Seidensticker then slowly turned to the young lady on his right, and drawled, "That was a very nice cat."

Boy with Cat was by no means a great film, but it was a noble experiment, the work of a foreign romantic who had found his corner of paradise. Donald had none of Oshima's political radicalism; he was too detached for that. Nor did he especially admire Oshima's films, which I think he found didactic. Donald much preferred the movies of Ozu Yasujiro, whose quiet, humanistic fatalism was everything that Oshima's generation rebelled against. And yet, in a profound sense, Richie and Oshima were on the same side.

Far from producing anything of my own, I was still at the stage of deciphering what I heard and saw. I spent hours trying to make sense of essays by Terayama Shuji with the help of a dictionary, imagining that my guesswork somehow added something to the mystique of what I was reading. His most famous essay encouraged young people to leave home, move to the city, and love freely. But Terayama himself lived the wild life mostly in his imagination. The same was true for me.

Theater performances were especially hard to crack. One summer night I saw Kara Juro's Jokyo Gekijo (Situation Theater) perform in a crimson tent pitched on the edge of a large pond in Ueno, the water surface covered in pink lotus flowers. Kara's troupe was another legend of the sixties. Like traveling players in premodern Japan, Kara and his actors put up their tent all over Japan, at Shinto shrines, between railway tracks, in abandoned car parks, on fairgrounds, and on riverbanks. His plays were surreal collages drawn from Japanese as well as Western sources, sometimes melodramatic, always raucous, and full of wild humor, acted in a loud, exaggerated, stylized manner that owed something to the bawdy origins of Kabuki, and something to the rough-and-ready style of cross-talking comedians. They were as deliberately grotesque as Terayama's spectacles, but earthier, more physical. Actors would suddenly appear drenched from a tank of water, or from a pond behind the tent. A spectacular entrance by one of the main stars would be greeted by wild cheers from the audience pressed together on straw mats.

The play I saw on that humid night in 1975, entitled *Kaze no Matasaburo,* was based on a Japanese fairy tale about a wind sprite appearing from nowhere as a student at a small village school in the rural northeast. Kara combined this with a variation of the Orpheus myth: a mother searching for her long-lost son in the underworld. Songs, or zany references to popular movies, manga characters, TV commercials, political scandals, and even snatches of French existentialism alternated with scenes of pure slapstick.

I understood virtually nothing. But the effect was similar to what I had experienced at the Mickery Theater in Amsterdam. I was transported into a strange new place, as disturbing as it was seductive, which looked no less strange when the flaps of the red tent opened at the end to reveal the moonlit lotus pond in all its uncanny glory. The state of mystification during my first year in Japan, deciphering words, codes, and signs, and only half-understanding them, as I wandered through the maze of modern Tokyo, felt strangely akin to the spirit of Kara's plays, with its lost characters trying to connect in a surreal world.

I began my story by claiming that I felt no attraction to the exotic. And this was true, as far as Zen meditation or some of the finer arts were concerned. But I was fascinated by the outlandish aspects of Japanese culture, the *ero, guro, nansensu*. And the erotic, the grotesque, and the absurd continue to intrigue me, even though much of their physical manifestations are more hidden now under ever-slicker layers of Japanese modernity.

My chief guide into the mysteries of Japanese culture, apart from Donald, my sensei, was a dropout student named Tsuda. A small man with a fringed Beatles haircut, Tsuda was one of those people whose intellectual brilliance took him everywhere and nowhere. Endlessly curious, always ready with an interesting theory, Tsuda was stimulating company. But in conventional terms he would have to be classified as a failure. He viewed a university education as a waste of time, and competing for a decent job to be beneath his dignity. With just enough family funds to keep him afloat, Tsuda was a flaneur, a dabbler, a dreamer, and above all, a talker. He could talk about anything: Oshima's movies, traditional Japanese architecture, Nietzsche, nineteenth-century Romantic literature, or the decadence of Japanese aesthetics. An extra boon to me was the fact that he couldn't speak a word of English.

We first met while standing in line for tickets to see Suzuki Tadashi's theater company perform a play that mixed Greek drama with a smattering of texts by the mid-nineteenth-century Kabuki playwright Tsuruya Namboku. We hit it off, Tsuda and I, because it soon became clear that we were both outsiders in different ways. He had made himself an outsider from the inside, as it were, whereas I was peering in from the outside. We were both voyeurs really, exploring the proletarian east of the city, hanging around the cheap cafés and bars in Shinjuku, and meeting up with his cronies from Tokyo University, who had not dropped out, who had found good jobs, and whom Tsuda regarded with a mixture of pride and disdain, except perhaps for one, named Nasu, whom he admired without reservation. After completing a law degree, Nasu had made a successful career at Nikkatsu making *roman porno* movies.

I never succeeded in making a student film at Nichidai, even though I did acquire an 8mm camera, the standard tool for student productions. Instead I used the excellent darkroom facilities and concentrated on photography, the perfect art for a voyeur dancing around the fringes. Japan, especially then, was a photographer's dream. Before photography entered the artistic mainstream elsewhere, photographers were celebrated figures in Japan whose shows at major galleries were mobbed by crowds of enthusiasts. Among the Japanese texts I was trying to decipher were the thick, glossy, deeply serious photography magazines, published by large newspaper companies. Moriyama Daido, who would become world famous decades later, gave evening classes in a tiny space in Shinjuku, which I sometimes attended, dipping in and out, hovering at the edges. Shinoyama Kishin was taking pictures of tattooed gangsters, fashion models, and a rising young Kabuki star, named Tamasaburo, who specialized in female roles. The seedy backstreets of U.S. base towns were recorded in grainy black and white by Tomatsu Shomei.

And then there was Araki. He was everywhere in the 1970s, making the rounds of the tiny bars in Shinjuku, or the raunchiest cabarets, giggling and chattering nonstop, as he snapped away at anything that caught his fancy on the seamy side of Tokyo nightlife: cabaret hostesses cavorting in the nude amid drunken punters in suits, naked girls eating bananas or pissing into plastic umbrellas held up by grinning patrons, women tied up in ropes or being fucked in live sex shows.

The wild seventies were sometimes called Showa Genroku, after the hedonistic Genroku Period at the end of the seventeenth century. (Showa was the name of Emperor Hirohito's reign, which spanned much of the twentieth century.) Araki's face, with the tiny round spectacles, the dirty old man's moustache, and the intense little voyeur's eyes, had become one of the icons of Showa Genroku. He was the Toulouse-Lautrec of contemporary *ero, guro, nansensu*.

Photographers were doing what woodblock-print artists had done in premodern Japan, chronicling the floating world of fashion, theater, sex, and urban life. One facet of sixties culture that lingered in the seventies was a fascination for what Japanese call *dorokusai,* which means stinking of the earth, or *nostalgie de la boue.* The seedy, the obscene, the debauched, the bloody, the smelly, all that permeated the arts scene, not just in photography, but in theater, film, literature, manga, and even the graphic arts. It was, I think, a reaction to elite aesthetics, which, since the mid-nineteenth century, was either rigidly traditionalist or a prissy Japanese version of European high culture.

Mishima once wrote, in an introduction to a book of photographs of frenzied young men at rowdy Shinto festivals taken by Tex Weatherby's lover Yato Tamotsu, that late nineteenth century Japan had become ashamed of its popular culture, afraid that Westerners would be shocked by its earthiness. Japan, he wrote, "tried to deny her past completely, or at least to hide from Western eyes any of the old ways that might resist all efforts to eradicate them. The Japanese were like an anxious housewife preparing to receive guests, hiding away in closets common articles of daily use and laying aside comfortable everyday clothes, hoping to impress the guests with the immaculate, idealized life of her household, without so much as a speck of dust in view."*

The trend in the sixties, continuing into the seventies, went in the opposite direction. Even though many Japanese of the wartime and early postwar generations had deeply ambivalent feelings about Westerners, the idea was not to eradicate Western influence. That would have been impossible, indeed absurd. But artists like Terayama, Kara, Oshima, Araki, and indeed Mishima wanted to strip Japanese culture of that

---

* *Naked Festival: A Photo-Essay,* Tokyo: Weatherhill, 1968.

thick crust of gentility, formed over many decades of anxious Westernization.

My own *nostalgie de la boue* had less to do with Japanese attitudes toward the West than with my protected background. My immersion in Japan was also partly a flight from bourgeois gentility, even if this flight was superficial, voyeuristic, semi-detached. I photographed the backstreets of Shinjuku, in the style of Moriyama Daido, who got much of his inspiration from the American William Klein, and I roamed around the still raffish areas flanking the Sumida River in the eastern lowlands, the so-called *shitamachi,* or low city, as opposed to the high city in the more prosperous hilly areas of the west.

My preferred part of Tokyo, to wander through and photograph, ran from Minami Senju, where a small neglected cemetery under the railway tracks marks the old Edo Period execution grounds, through Sanya, the skid row, where labor contractors picked up homeless men for cheap construction jobs every morning, thence on to Yoshiwara, once the elegant red-light district of high-class brothels and teahouses, and now a sordid warren of neon-lit massage parlors, and finally to the temple in Asakusa dedicated to Kannon, the goddess of mercy.

My literary guide on these wanderings was one of my favorite Japanese writers, named Nagai Kafu, who died in 1959. His subject was Tokyo, his temperament elegiac. The vulgarity of the present disgusted him. Kafu (he was always known by this sobriquet) could only love in retrospect, and celebrate what had disappeared. The Westernized city of the late nineteenth and early twentieth century Meiji Period moved him deeply only after it had been largely destroyed by the 1923 earthquake. The brassy modern Tokyo that emerged after that disaster filled him with delight, but only after it was wrecked by B-29 bombers in 1945. Kafu was a mournful archaeologist of the recent past: the tiled wall of a former 1930s brothel in the midst of a crassly modernized postwar neighborhood could move him to tears.

There was an old tumbledown theater in Minami Senju with luridly hand-painted pictures outside of sword-waving warriors and moonfaced geishas. This theater, smelling of fried squid and stale sweat, was home to one of the last troupes of traveling players, who performed crude versions of famous Kabuki plays about love suicides and noble outlaws. In between acts, the players, after quickly changing into bright Hawaiian shirts, would belt out popular songs through faltering microphones, while others twanged on badly tuned electric guitars. All the female roles were performed by men in the traditional style. One of the actors, a snub-nosed young man with rubbery, rather coarse features, managed, in his female guise, to look beautiful even in these squalid surroundings. Twenty years later he became a national celebrity, appearing on TV as the "low city Tamasaburo," after the famous Kabuki actor.

I spent many hours in the Minami Senju theater, taking pictures of the actors, and of the public whose average age must have been well over fifty: the local butcher and his stocky wife, a petty crook or two, roof builders, construction workers, and dumpling cooks. God only knows what they thought of the young foreigner snapping away at their feet. But they were always welcoming in a politely amused sort of way.

One weekend, I followed the actors on one of their rural tours, with Graham, my friend from the Nichidai library. We stayed the night at a seedy hot spring resort, called a "Green Center," where old folks would gather to drink and be entertained by the low city Tamasaburo and his fellow players. We sat at long wooden tables laden with rice balls, dried squid, pickles, and miso soup, dressed in thin summer kimonos provided by the Green Center, watching a blood-curdling scene of murder committed by a famous nineteenth-century brigand, followed by a famous love scene from a creaky samurai drama. All the while, I was creeping around taking pictures in the way I had seen Araki do. But the main entertainment was yet to come.

When it was time for a soak in the large communal bath, men and women shed their summer wear, and beckoned Graham and me to come in too. The tiled bathroom had the sulphurous stench of rotten eggs. Mount Fuji on the wall was half obscured by steam coming off the scalding hot water. After a quick wash, Graham and I slid gingerly into the bath, with all eyes on us. We could not have been more immersed in deepest Japan, I thought, when all of a sudden a burst of cackling laughter creased the wrinkled country faces around us. "Look at those pricks!" one of the oldest ladies in the bath shrieked, "Look at those foreigners' pricks!" "They're bigger than yours, Granddad!" shouted a stout woman who must have been at least eighty. Several shriveled old men smiled sheepishly. "Ooh, aren't gaijin white!" a third lady exclaimed, as though she had never seen anything so grotesque in her life, "just like tofu."

Not long after this excursion to the Green Center, I came across another group of entertainers, even lower down the social scale. Tsuda and I had set off on a cold November night, during the Tori-no-Ichi, or Day of the Rooster, the harvest

Actor in the theater at Minami Senju

festival when for twelve days street markets are laid out near temples and shrines, where people pray for a prosperous new year, buy talismanic bamboo rakes decorated with rice and flowers, and eat a special kind of sweet potato said to boost human fertility. This is where "the Human Pump" had set up his brown-and-green-striped carnival tent, featuring such curiosities as "the snake woman," whose neck appeared to grow all the way to the top of the tent, the girl who bit off the heads of live chickens, and the hairy wolf man.

The carnival tent was erected in the same spot where Kara Juro's company often pitched their red tent, in front of Hanazono Shrine, dedicated to Inari, the androgynous fox deity of prosperity and worldly success. People craned their necks to see the shrieking young woman hold a chicken in her teeth, her shiny face smeared with blood and feathers and illuminated by a flaming torch. There was a strange ghostly sound of a whistle as the snake woman's neck got longer and longer. And the wolf man barked at the crowd, which retreated in mock terror.

But the main act was the leader of the troupe, the Human Pump himself. He was an albino male of about forty. The words "human pump" were written in Japanese phonetic script on his dark sweater. First he would swallow a number of shiny black and white buttons. The public was asked to call out "white" or "black," whereupon the Human Pump would blink his tiny pale eyes and spit out a button of the requisite color. But his pièce de résistance was the goldfish act. He would swallow a live orange goldfish, then a yellow one, and shake his head a few times, like the fish-eating cormorants I had seen on a river in western Japan, to let them slide smoothly through his gullet.

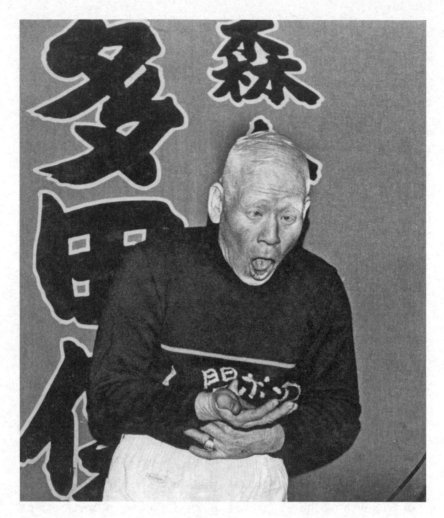

The Human Pump

"Orange!" cried the crowd, and slowly with intense concentration, the right goldfish would come jetting out of his mouth.

These were modest skills, perhaps. Seen from backstage, the trick with the elongated neck became apparent when I noticed the girl's lower body made up of bamboo and papier-mâché. I'm still not sure how the Human Pump managed to regurgitate the different colored objects on demand. But there was something about the carnival show that mesmerized me, its rawness, its primitive appeal. Here, I thought, was performance reduced to the most basic elements. I realized that this had everything to do with my bourgeois romanticism, my *nostalgie de la boue*. It was nothing more than a peek into a strange world, a voyeur's glimpse of the forbidden. But I couldn't get enough of it. So I followed the Human Pump and his family around (the snake woman was his wife, the chicken girl their adopted daughter, and the wolf man was a brother-in-law, I think), taking pictures backstage, congratulating myself on my brush with the theatrical underworld, the absolute "Other," as illusory no doubt as Donald Richie's dreams of "innocence," even if I did not realize that yet. Before they left Tokyo to tour other shrines in the provinces, the Human Pump handed me his name card. "Come and look us up sometime," he said. The address was in a small town not far from Gifu, where the Tani family lived.

Unfortunately I have no photographic record of the most remarkable performance I saw in the summer of 1976. This was not in Tokyo, which had stricter laws about permissible entertainments than other cities, possibly as a result of having to look respectable, like Mishima's prim housewife, for the Tokyo Olympics in 1964. The Toji Deluxe was in Kyoto, behind the main railway station, near the old designated area for outcasts, or *burakumin,* who did ritually unclean work connected with death, such as butchering, tanning, meat packing, or, in the olden days, executing prisoners. The Toji's flashing neon lights were the only bright spot in an otherwise dark street.

The girl who bit the chicken's neck

In the middle of a huge barn-like space was a round, slowly revolving stage, with men sitting in rows waiting for the action to start. Tsuda and I were in the second row. Precisely on time, the theater went dark and a soft pink light suffused the stage. A young man in a shiny electric-blue suit and purple bow tie appeared with a chrome microphone, and loudly welcomed us to the show, his words echoing spookily through the theater. The performers were introduced by name, as they shuffled onto the stage carrying plastic picnic hampers neatly covered in bits of cloth with pictures of various cartoon characters, Snoopy and the like. I saw one of them hand a baby to one of the stage-hands, as she made her entrance. Frank Sinatra's "Strangers in the Night" issued forth from the scratchy sound system.

The girls, dressed in negligees, made a bow and simpered in unison—what a pleasure it was to entertain us honorable guests tonight. They crouched down, removed the cloth from their baskets, and carefully laid out various props on the edge of the stage: vibrators of different sizes, in pink, yellow, and violet, as well as cucumbers, and condoms wrapped in colored cellophane packages. Everything was done with the utmost decorum, the props placed in neat little rows, "Strangers in the Night" still playing.

They stood up and adopted a number of suggestive poses, their faces as mask-like as Noh dancers or Bunraku puppets. The men in the audience were a mixture of old and young, some dressed in suits and ties, as though coming straight from the office, some dressed like students, a few of them with sports bags. Some of the older men wore the uniforms of Japanese workers, wide khaki trousers, thick woolen waistbands, black splay-toed canvas shoes.

On the revolving stage, a few of the girls broke into friendly smiles and slowly made their way to the edge, where the condoms and other props were laid out. One or two picked up a dildo or a cucumber and entered several transparent square boxes that were cranked up a little noisily over our heads. An old-fashioned Japanese ballad began to play on the sound system, something about a lonely mother waiting for her son to come back from abroad. Tsuda whispered in my ear that it was a wartime song.

"Now watch closely," said Tsuda, who was an old hand at these things. One by one, the girls onstage moved to the edge and beckoned men in the audience to come forward and join them. Meanwhile, above us, in the transparent buckets, girls were busy inserting cucumbers and dildos into their vaginas.

The men giggled and dared one another to climb up. A thin man in a business suit was pushed forward by his friends, but he refused to go, blushing furiously, and scratching the back of his neck, the common Japanese gesture for embarrassment. Finally, one of the students, in sneakers and training pants, went up. He stood up straight, like a soldier on parade, staring blankly ahead, while a girl, smiling sweetly, took off all his clothes except for a pair of white sports socks. She expertly slipped on a condom and lay down invitingly. "The doors of paradise are about to open, gentlemen," said the emcee in the purple bow tie. Shouts of encouragement came from the audience. The young man, without looking at the girl, began to make vigorous movements with his hips.

Alas, the tension must have got to him. Tsuda told me that students often save up for these occasions, sex being relatively unavailable to them otherwise. The young man began to sweat, the girl made soft cooing noises, telling him it would be OK. But after a last hopeless shake of his hips, the young man gave up. Older men in the audience chortled at the boy's failure. The girl patted his back, as he scrambled off the stage still in his white socks with his trousers pulled halfway up his thighs.

So was this it? I asked my friend. He motioned with the palm of his hand in a calming gesture: "Just wait and see." The emcee made another announcement through his mike: "Honored guests, the time has come for the *tokudashi*." "The *tokudashi*?" I asked Tsuda. "Just wait." The emcee, breathing heavily into his mike, said in English: "Open."

The men in the audience, as though waiting for this climactic moment, moved forward, wide-eyed, as three women sitting at the very edge of the stage leaned back on their elbows and very slowly opened their legs, exposing themselves to the prying gaze of the fascinated audience. The emcee handed out some magnifying glasses and small hand torches. "Please share them around, so everyone can have a proper look," he said.

There was a deadly hush in the theater. No chortling or cackling now, as the women moved sideways like crabs from man to man, each taking his turn to peer into the female mystery with the help of torch and magnifying glass. The women encouraged the men to take their time. I was riveted by the spectacle no less than I had been when I first saw Terayama's theater or Kara's play in the red tent. Here was a world that was both deeply strange and utterly human, like some primitive ritual.

After it was all over, Tsuda and I had a drink in a tiny bar near the station. He had a theory about the spectacle we had just witnessed. Japan, he explained, still had vestiges of an ancient matriarchy. In Shinto, he continued, the sun is venerated as a mother goddess, named Amaterasu. One day, according to legend, the sun goddess retreated into a cave in a fit of anger. The world was cast in darkness and evil spirits roamed. The other gods, worried about this state of affairs, tried to coax her out. But Amaterasu stubbornly refused. They tried every trick: roosters were made to crow, pretending it was dawn; a tree covered in jewels and a bronze mirror was placed in front of the cave. Still, she didn't stir. Then the goddess of mirth and revelry, named Ama no Uzume, began to dance wildly on top of a wooden tub, stamping her feet and lifting her dress to show off her private parts, whereupon the gods burst out laughing. The sun goddess could no longer contain her curiosity, peeked out of her hiding place, and was so taken by her own reflection in the mirror on the tree that the gods were able to drag her out, so light came into the world once more.

This Tsuda told me, and much more, before we parted ways at Kyoto station, Tsuda to go back to Tokyo, and me to the small town not too far away where I was hoping to visit the Human Pump and his family. I don't know what I imagined their daily life to be like: a kind of carnival, perhaps living in a romantic wooden shack or even a tent with other carnies and geeks. I could picture them practicing swallowing swords and goldfish or crying like wolves.

Since Japanese addresses follow no logic, I had some difficulty finding their house. But I did in the end. It was an ordinary modern house with a blue-tiled roof, like millions of others, on a rather dreary suburban street. The Human Pump, dressed in khaki trousers and a plaid shirt, welcomed me in and offered tea and sweet rice cakes. We made small talk about the weather, the difficulty of recent tax hikes, and the bother of traveling. The television was on all the while, with the sound turned down. Wolf man, without his costume, was a rather taciturn figure in a thick gray sweater. The snake woman kept offering me more cakes, until I really couldn't manage any more. And the chicken-eating girl asked me about Alain Delon, whom she adored, as did millions of other young Japanese women, assuming, perhaps, that as a fellow gaijin I would have special knowledge of her idol.

They couldn't have been nicer. Yet I couldn't help feeling a little deflated. The mystery had gone. There was no absolute

Other. I had not penetrated the murky depths of some secret world. My romance had been punctured, a little.

So was my immersion an illusion? Not entirely. It was our common humanity, after all, that had attracted me to Japanese films when I first saw them in Europe. And common humanity is what I found in the middle-class household of the albino goldfish swallower. As with so many ordinary families, the placid surface may have hidden all kinds of secret strangeness. If so, I didn't see it here. My illusion was to suppose that strangeness lies on the surface. But then it was Donald, my sensei, who often impressed me with the notion that "the Japanese" never assume hidden depths. "They take the surface seriously," he would say. "The package is the substance. That is at the heart of their sense of beauty."

Perhaps he was right. Surfaces matter. One of the things I had tried to imitate in Japan was the style of dress of people I thought looked cool. There was a fashion among young people in the seventies to wear traditional wooden Japanese sandals, or *geta*, especially in the summer. *Geta* are meant to be worn with a kimono, but young men sported them with jeans. They are made of a wooden block, with a thong made of cloth. A few really hip young men would wear the more dandyish high *geta*, normally worn by fishmongers and others who need to rise above wet and slippery floors. The *takageta* had super high heels, making it look as if the wearer were walking on low stilts.

I wore *takageta*, of course, tottering around the narrow shopping streets of Tokyo with the loud satisfying clip-clop of wood on tarmac, feeling very Japanese. This was part of my immersion. Until one day, on a visit to my relative's mansion in

Aobadai, where I had stayed during my first month in Tokyo, I clip-clopped my way to the gate of his house. There were quite a few people in the street, including some of my relative's staff who had instructed me on Japanese ways. Suddenly, with a hideous crack of shattering wood, I felt my footwear give way, and there I was, with one *geta* still on, limping to the door. Nobody laughed. They were much too polite for that. In fact, everyone pretended not to have seen a thing.

FOUR

For Donald Richie, growing up in Lima, Ohio, must have been a torment. A small industrial midwestern town, where the influence of the KKK still lingered, was no place for an artistic young gay boy, hungry for adventure. His only escape was the Sigma movie theater, where a wider world opened up to him. He once wrote that Norma Shearer and Johnny Weissmuller felt more like parents than his real ones. In his words: "In the dusty dark of the Sigma I was content, at home more than I ever was at home."*

Terayama Shuji grew up in the remote northeast of Japan, the thick accent of which he retained, indeed perhaps cultivated, even after years of living in Tokyo. His father had died as a soldier in the war. His mother was usually away, working in a bar at a U.S. military base. Relatives took care of him. They owned a cinema. It was there, doing his homework behind the film screen, that Terayama grew up, hearing the same ghostly voices as Richie in Ohio. That dream palace, "smelling

---

* Arturo Silva, ed., *The Donald Richie Reader,* Berkeley: Stone Bridge Press, 2001.

of piss," was a recurring theme in Terayama's poems and plays. His fantasies had fed my fantasies. His was the circus that I followed out of my native country.

Donald's great escape came at the end of the war when he joined the merchant navy. His favorite book at the time was a baroque travel account entitled *The Asiatics,* by Frederic Prokosch. It described the travels of a young man from Beirut to China. Since Prokosch had never been anywhere east of Berlin, the book was an invention, made up by the author from guidebooks and travel stories. Donald actually met Prokosch, in 1945 or 1946. His merchant navy ship was moored in Naples, where Prokosch happened to be spending the winter. The writer, dressed in an elegant cream-colored suit, eyed the ship's crew, and selected some of the more fetching sailors for an evening on the town. Donald was one of them. Prokosch took a shine to him and wanted to know all about his rough life at sea. Donald answered by declaring how much he admired Prokosch's writing, whereupon the great man of letters rolled his eyes and turned away in disgust.

Donald left the merchant marine and applied for a job in Japan, which he got because of his peculiar talent for typing at great speed. Arriving in Tokyo in 1947, he began writing for the *Stars and Stripes* military newspaper; Japan was still under U.S. occupation. There were strict rules against "fraternizing" with the "indigenous personnel." Nightclubs, bars, cinemas, coffee shops, even the Kabuki theater, were off limits. Anyone caught sneaking into these indigenous spots could be sent back home in disgrace. Donald took the risk. He couldn't imagine living without the movies, and he wanted to be where the natives were.

One of his preferred haunts was the old Rokkuza Theater, which still stood in the ruins of Asakusa, in the midst of hastily rebuilt striptease parlors, all-girl operas, and burlesque houses. There he was, "wedged at the back, smelling the rice-odor sweat of the people back then, mixed with the fragrance of the camellia oil pomade the men used to use on their hair, and beyond these, the beloved odor of the vast, cold, dusty expectant emptiness in the back of the screen. Then the lights went down."

The movies for Donald were perhaps not a substitute for life, as they had been in Ohio. But they offered a glimpse into an entirely Japanese world. He couldn't understand a word of what was being said on the screen, but this, he believed, was partly to his advantage. It forced him to pay more attention to what he was taking in with his eyes. If he couldn't follow the stories, he could at least try to make sense of how they were told. He noticed the lack of close-up shots, compared with Hollywood movies, and he observed the body language of the characters seen in the middle distance. He was struck by the use of space in the way shots were composed, leaving much to the imagination, a bit like traditional Chinese-style paintings.

Thirty-odd years later, the smell of rice and camellia pomade had gone. But many of the old movie houses, in Asakusa, and other parts of Tokyo, were still there. Some were hidden in back alleys, some in underground shopping arcades, and some on the top floors of department stores. Tokyo in the 1970s was one of the world's great cinema cities, its offerings as varied as in New York or even Paris. There were dozens of art cinemas featuring new movies or retrospectives of Antonioni, Oshima, or Fellini. The latest Hollywood films, as well as commercial Japanese films, were shown in hundreds of cinemas scattered all over town. And then there were the seedier venues, offering all-night showings of Japanese gangster pictures, *roman porno,* or samurai epics in a haze of stale cigarette smoke.

My own attraction to the reek of mud drew me to the yakuza all-nighters, starring Takakura Ken or Tsuruta Koji. Ken-san bore a remarkable resemblance to the rugged country boys in Donald's private pinup collection. These films followed a predictable format, observed with the solemnity of a religious rite: the hero, provoked by intolerable humiliations meted out by the bad guys, would always die alone in a final scene of mayhem. Toei studios, which had strong connections to real yakuza gangs, were the main producers of these movies. Mobsters tend to be conservative. The bad guys were crooked bankers, corrupt politicians, or greedy construction bosses. They wore pinstriped business suits with flashy ties. Ken-san and other yakuza heroes wore kimonos. They were the last real warriors, faithful to the ancient codes of chivalry: loyalty, self-sacrifice, and justice. They fought with swords against the cowardly bad hats who invariably fought with guns.

The politics of the classic yakuza movie were not so much right wing as aggressively antimodern. A pure, traditional Japan, which was almost wholly fictional, was being corrupted by modern capitalism and Western ways. This caricature of history goes back to the mid-nineteenth century, when U.S. gunships forced Japan out of her state of relative isolation. Then the helter-skelter economic boom of the 1960s, as well as bruised feelings about the years of U.S. occupation, gave the fantasy a new life. Which is why Ken-san, an essentially reactionary hero, was an idol to left-wing student protesters too. They also longed for a pure society, which could only exist in myth.

Without having the same yearnings as the student activists of the 1960s, I, too, felt the pull of the yakuza myth, which in its classical form was already a thing of the past. Japanese gangster pictures, like American Westerns, which in many respects they resembled, had become darker, more cynical, by the 1970s. Perhaps my taste for the earlier films had something to do with the attempt to flee from my own background, but I think there was more to it than that. Who, with any romantic sense at all, would not root for the men in kimonos against the men in suits, for the swords against the guns? The lament in the classic yakuza picture was the universal one, for paradise lost.

And so I, too, cheered lustily when Ken-san slipped his samurai sword from his waistband, and set off, alone, to face certain death at the hands of his enemies' guns. The suicidal mission would be accompanied by a rousing song on the sound track, usually sung by the hero himself, celebrating the beauty of death as a final act of vengeance against the corrupt Westernized villains. The kamikaze spirit still lingered, thirty years after the war. Even the sleeping bums would wake up for the climax and shout at the screen: "Go, Ken-san! Die like a man!"

I SOON DECIDED that my Japanese cinema education was not best served by the Nichidai art school. Even though I continued to use the darkrooms for my photography, I no longer attended the film classes, even those of Sentimental Ushihara. Instead, as Donald had done before me in the wreckage of bombed-out

Tokyo, I immersed myself in the Japanese imagination as a re-flection of Japanese life. That is to say, I spent much of my time in the cinema.

My school, in this enterprise, was the National Film Center, a banal white-tiled building tucked away under a flyover near the Kyobashi underground railway station. Donald had intro-duced me to the kindly curators who ran the place. One of them, Shimizu-san, had worked for a Japanese production company in Shanghai during the war, specializing in Chinese movies that complied with the aims of the Japanese military occupation, without descending to crude propaganda. Shimizu seemed like a dour fellow, until he had a few cups of his beloved sake. He would get giggly and red in the face, and tell stories about the good old days in occupied Shanghai.

Shimizu idolized the man who ran the wartime studio, named Kawakita Nagamasa, a legendary figure in the Japanese film world, who together with his wife, Kashiko, distributed European films in Japan before the war and continued to pro-mote Japanese movies abroad. His genuine sympathy for the Chinese invited the distrust of Japanese military officials in Shanghai during the 1940s. There were rumors of attempts made on his life by thugs employed by the Japanese secret service.

I would occasionally catch a glimpse of Kawakita floating around the Film Center, a dapper silver-haired man in beauti-fully cut charcoal-gray suits. His reputation as a ladies' man still hung about him, like a faint odor of expensive perfume. But his wife, Kashiko, was more often in attendance, very much the grande dame, always dressed in understated kimonos. She was not only a regular at the Film Center but also at almost every private film screening in town. Her manners were so fine that one felt boorish in her presence. After stoically enduring yet another "youth film" about young men in leather jackets and sunglasses, she would smile politely, tilt her beautifully coiffed head in a half bow, and declare that it was "a splendid motion picture," without having the slightest intention of promoting it.

There is something a little creepy about film buffs living the imaginary lives of others vicariously in the dark. Tsuda sometimes came with me to the Film Center. And sometimes my companion was a Greek film student named Vassilis, a pale-faced man with fleshy cheeks, who had a passion for the films of Mizoguchi Kenji. He talked of little else, when his attention wasn't drawn to some miniskirted girl passing by, which would elicit soft moaning noises, like a dog pining after his lunch. Vassilis would hold forth at great length on Mizoguchi's silent films, or on that famous tracking shot in *The Life of Oharu* (1952), when the fallen woman, played by Tanaka Kinuyo, tries to see her long-lost son at the mansion of a nobleman whose mistress she had once been. Vassilis could even mimic the sound of the bamboo flutes playing court music at the end of *Ugetsu* (1953).

For a long time I would attend screenings at the Film Center every afternoon, and sometimes the evenings too. There were retrospectives of Ozu's great films, as well as Kurosawa's. I discovered for myself the masterpieces of Naruse Mikio, a still underrated director, whose bleak stories of lonely bar hostesses and women longing in vain to escape from suffocating marriages moved me as deeply as Ozu's family dramas. The slyly subversive comedies by Kinoshita Keisuke were shown, as well as more unusual series: on the remarkably good wartime Japanese propaganda films, or the silent films of the 1920s, which were as interesting as the German expressionist movies that frequently inspired them. The wonderful films I had read about in Donald Richie's books were no longer just names. They flickered into life one by one on the top floor of that dreary building in Kyobashi.

The movies covered every aspect of Japanese society, but one subject appeared to dominate all else in art films: the often melancholy role of women—heroic, self-sacrificing mothers, kind-hearted prostitutes, women caught in hopeless love affairs ending in romantic suicides. This interest might seem incongruous in a country where women's emancipation was so slow in coming. Perhaps male guilt had something to do with it. Mizoguchi Kenji, himself a frequent visitor of brothels in Tokyo and Kyoto, once stood in front of a roomful of prostitutes at a VD clinic, apologized for what men had done to them, and broke down in tears.

As a regular at the Film Center I soon came to recognize my fellow dwellers in the dark. They were an odd bunch who turned up at every screening: a thin, older man, always dressed in a white cowboy hat and a bolo tie; a dandyish baby-faced figure who wore a pearl tiepin with his dove-gray suits, like a 1920s movie star; a short dumpy man in his forties who looked a bit like a tramp, with long greasy hair and a grubby denim jacket with the words "I am Japanese hippy" stenciled on the back. They invariably sat in the same seats in the second row, unless some hapless film fan had inadvertently taken one of their places, which would result in muttered complaints in the hallway.

I don't think they were close friends. After the screenings, each would go his way. But inside the cinema they were inseparable. Between films, they would huddle in the corridor, recalling different scenes from favorite movies. Bits of dialogue were rehearsed, and opinions exchanged about this actor or that one. The last scene in Ozu's *Late Spring* (1949), in which Ryu Chishu plays the father left alone after his only daughter's wedding, was dissected frame by frame. Sometimes there would be soft bickering about the merits of one performance over another.

I didn't join this select company, but as usual I hovered around the edges, listening in. I never knew their names, and they certainly didn't know mine. But somehow the rumor had reached them that I was related to John Schlesinger. This had the disconcerting consequence that every time I entered the screening room, I saw heads in the second row turn in my direction with whisperings of "Shulesinjaa."

I think that Ryu Chishu, or Tanaka Kinuyo, or to be more precise, the imaginary characters they portrayed, were more real to the film buffs than any existing human being. This is why cinephiles are spookier, on the whole, than music lovers or balletomanes. For they are creatures of the dark, getting off on the lives of others.

But of course I was one of them. I, too, was absorbed in Japanese lives imagined by writers and directors in the golden age of Japanese cinema. I loved the three greats, of course: Ozu, Mizoguchi, and Kurosawa. Some say that one cannot love all three equally, since they are so different in style and temperament: Ozu's Zen-like minimalism, Mizoguchi's lush and painterly Japanese aesthetics, and Kurosawa's technical genius, owing something to fast Hollywood-style cutting as well as to the drama of classical Japanese theater.

Ozu is often regarded as the most "Japanese" of the three, so much so that his studio refused to distribute his films abroad at first, assuming that gaijin would never understand them, and perhaps even laugh at Japanese in Western suits sipping tea on tatami floors. Kurosawa was sometimes criticized for "reeking of butter," a Japanese expression for people or things that have a phony Western air. Even as a raw film student, I realized that this was nonsense. Kurosawa, the only one of the three still alive in the 1970s, was resented for his success outside Japan. He was the proverbial nail that stuck out, so critics did their best to hammer it back in.

Some Western movie lovers treated Japanese cinema as a kind of cult. One of these enthusiasts was a Frenchman named Max Tessier. Japanese films were almost like a fetish for him. His knowledge rivaled that of the cinematic vampires at the Film Center. But when asked why he had become so engrossed in Japanese films, to the exclusion of almost all else, without even speaking Japanese or ever having lived in Japan for any length of time, he would get irritated, as though one had asked a homosexual why he liked sleeping with men. He spoke of his passion as if it were a biological necessity.

I think I can explain my own infatuation with films from the Japanese golden age, running from the 1930s to the 1960s, after which television ruined the studio system and great Japanese films became ever more rare. What the movies made by Ozu,

Mizoguchi, Kurosawa, Naruse, and many other lesser-known directors had in common was an emotional realism. They approached the darker human impulses, sexual, social, spiritual, with a rare honesty less often seen in European or American films. This was not just the result of a lucky confluence of cinematic geniuses. Japanese audiences played an important role too. They were receptive to emotional realism. This seems to be less true today. I am not sure why. Perhaps because even the memories of shared hardships and deprivations are fading.

Donald once wrote about Kurosawa that heroes in his films were never just being, but always in the state of becoming. The remark stuck in my mind, because it said as much about Donald as it did about Kurosawa's movies. It reminded me of what he told me about foreign romantics in Japan, the idea of the self as a work in progress, open-ended, embracing uncertainty. The subject of all great art, Donald also once said, is the nature of reality. This may be why Kurosawa was fanatical about getting details just right. Everything had to look real. The props for a film set in the sixteenth century had to be genuine, not fakes. For one of his films, *Throne of Blood* (1957), Kurosawa had a medieval castle built at huge expense, only to have it pulled down again when he noticed that nails had been used in the construction, an anachronism that the camera just might have detected. But all this belongs to the golden age, when the studios were making enough money to indulge their star directors. By the 1970s, those times were over. Kurosawa was finding it impossible to get money in Japan to make the films he wanted. In 1971 he tried to kill himself with a razor.

I witnessed Kurosawa's perfectionism at first hand eight

Kurosawa Akira with actors on
the set of *Kagemusha*

years later, when Donald and I were asked to appear as Portuguese missionaries in his film *Kagemusha*, despite the fact that
neither of us looked remotely Iberian. The movie was partly
financed by a Hollywood studio. Ours were not speaking roles.
We would barely even be glimpsed in a crowd scene. And yet,
as we were being made up and costumed for our roles, facing
the mirror in a cramped dressing room at the Toho studio,
Kurosawa spent a whole afternoon fussing about the way we
looked, the right amount of white powder in Donald's hair, the
precise cut of our Jesuit gowns. In the end, it was all for nothing. The minor roles were offered to two other foreigners.

But I did see Kurosawa shoot a battle scene for *Kagemusha*,
the sixteenth-century story of a criminal ordered to imperson-
ate a dying warlord to keep up the morale of his followers. In
his blue cap and dark glasses, Kurosawa towered over his crew,
arms folded and tight-lipped, his chin raised, like a general sur-
veying his troops. He waved his arm imperiously, and shouted:
"Prepare! Start!" Whereupon hundreds of samurai on horse-
back came charging down the hill, with the golden rays of the
afternoon sun filtered through the dust from the horses' hooves.
Kurosawa stamped his feet in disgust, and ordered his soldiers
to go back and do it all over again. Someone had ruined the shot
by waving a green battle flag a split second too soon.

I had met Kurosawa before, in 1976, at a private screening
of Stanley Kubrick's *Barry Lyndon*. When the lights went up,
the tall man in dark tinted glasses smiled politely when Madame
Kawakita introduced me as John Schlesinger's nephew, my only
rather dubious mark of distinction. He then spoke at some
length about the new 55mm lenses that Kubrick had used to

shoot his eighteenth-century interiors by candlelight. This was what he liked to talk about: technique, not theory. He hated being asked about the meaning of his films, for the work should speak for itself. He could explain technical details, about his multiple camera setups, or the particular film stock he used. But he had already talked about such things for so long. I watched him at press conferences, puffing smoke from his cigarette, barely able to conceal his impatience with questions he had heard too many times before. Japanese called him "the Emperor." Many people were frightened of him.

Apart from his films, Kurosawa once said, he didn't exist. He had to have a current project. Otherwise he might as well die. He was going through a fallow period in the late 1970s, waiting to get enough money to make *Kagemusha*. This made him especially irritable. To tide him over financially, he appeared in a number of commercials for Suntory whiskey. His most trusted assistant, a splendid lady named Nogami Teruyo, affectionately known as Non-chan, was the producer. She was perhaps the only person, other than himself, whose artistic judgment he trusted. He never shouted at her. She was like his talisman. Before every shot, Kurosawa would turn to Non-chan, standing beside the main camera, to ask her whether she thought it looked OK. One day, Non-chan called me to ask whether I would like to be in one of the whiskey commercials, together with Max Tessier, the French movie historian. We were to have a conversation with Kurosawa at his country house on the outer slopes of Mount Fuji.

Kurosawa was not enjoying himself, sitting up in his chair, smoking cigarettes, and giving orders to the cameraman about the right angle and proper lighting. The man who was formally in charge of directing the commercial broke into a nervous sweat every time Kurosawa gave directions to his crew. I turned to look out the window at the black volcanic landscape sloping toward the famous mountain in the distance. Max said something about the fine weather. Kurosawa grunted. I then asked him about a scene in *Seven Samurai* (1954). Kurosawa said: "Mmmm . . ."

Here we were in the presence of greatness, two European lovers of Japanese film, too tongue-tied to have a conversation with Kurosawa in a whiskey commercial. The movie lights were making me uncomfortably hot. Soon I, too, like the anxious director, was pouring with sweat. "Please talk," the director of the commercial whispered, casting a nervous glance at Kurosawa.

Kurosawa lit another cigarette, and waited, clutching a glass of amber barley tea in his right hand. Max asked him about *Throne of Blood*. Wasn't it shot on location near here? Kurosawa's eyes finally lit up behind his tinted glasses. Indeed it was, he said, and pointed at the black sand outside. That is where the castle had been, and where Mifune Toshiro was pierced on the ramparts by arrows shot into his armor at close range. As Kurosawa pointed out the camera positions for that famous last scene, and gestured with his hands to show how Mifune, in his role as a medieval Japanese Macbeth, slowly stumbled to his death, the movie landscape in the midst of which we were shooting the commercial came strangely alive. I could replay parts of the film in my mind, the grainy black-and-white landscape, the fog, the sound of the wind, and the look of horror in Mifune's eyes. It was almost as if the old castle loomed once again through the window. As for the commercial, I don't believe it was ever shown.

· · ·

ODDLY ENOUGH, I can't remember going to many film screenings with Donald. We spoke about the movies often but rarely saw them together. He certainly never came to the Film Center while I was there. But one particular movie house that we did visit together is still etched in my mind.

Donald lived in a tiny apartment on the top floor of an apartment building overlooking the Shinobazu no Ike, the pond with the lotus flowers where I first saw Kara Juro's Situation Theater perform in their red tent. The district, Ueno, is part of the plebeian *shitamachi,* or low city, where Donald felt more at home than in the wealthier hilly areas of Tokyo. Asakusa was not far off. A few minutes' walk from Donald's apartment building was a warren of alleys lined with neon-lit cabarets and louche massage parlors. Young pimps with frizzy haircuts and tattooed necks would hang about, trying to lure customers inside. Of a hot summer night, Donald liked to cruise in the small park bordering the lotus pond. Years later, Edward Seidensticker fell down the concrete steps leading to that same park and died of a skull fracture.

Near the park is a graceful old shrine, rebuilt many times since its inception in the fourteenth century, named Yushima Tenjin, after the spirit of a tenth-century poet, reincarnated as the god of thunder, lightning, and other natural disasters. But curiously enough, Tenjin was also the guardian deity of male love. There used to be male brothels clustered around the temple, and unlicensed Kabuki performances and gambling dens, all long gone.

The cinema Donald frequented regularly was located between this temple and his apartment building. It was one of the many movie houses specializing in *roman porno*. Posters of schoolgirls being ravaged by masked men, or of yakuza having their wicked ways with young housewives, flanked the ticket booth. You had to go down some steps to get inside. "Come," said Donald, like a gleeful cicerone, "you must see this."

I was slightly puzzled, since I would never have thought that Donald had any interest in films of this kind. The smell of rank sweat, urine, and harsh detergents was overpowering as we entered the dark corridor leading into the movie theater. The concrete floor felt slippery. Men went in and out of the public toilet, adjusting their trouser belts, trying to look casual, even as their eyes darted around as though in search of something.

It was hard to see anything inside the cinema at first. There was the loud noise of a woman panting in ecstasy. I turned toward the screen, where a man in dark glasses was pleasuring a respectable-looking lady with a dildo. Donald had disappeared. As my eyes got used to the gloom, I noticed that I was the only one paying any attention to the movie screen. For once, no one in the dream palace was living vicariously. There were men of all ages in every row of seats, in various states of undress, heaving and bobbing and clutching. The orgasmic noises coming from the movie screen failed to drown out the concert of sighs and grunts in the audience. I spotted Donald on the other side, a smile of deep contentment on his face.

After a while, I felt I had seen enough. "No, no," said my mentor, "wait till you see the toilets. There are peepholes in the stalls." No, I said, I really think I get the picture. With a slight air of disappointment, Donald took me outside into the dark and slippery corridor. And just at that moment a middle-aged man in a woman's dress appeared from the public restroom. His mouth was smudged with red lipstick. As soon as he recognized Donald, he lowered his head in a decorous bow, and said with enormous deference: "Sensei." There was not a hint of irony in his voice. He spoke with all the respect due to a great man of learning. Donald very politely bowed back.

Perhaps there was innocence after all.

FIVE

When Donald wasn't talking about movies, or the Japanese, at one of our regular coffee meetings, he talked about sex. The coffee shop near his place of work was popular with young women in prim office uniforms—knee-length gray skirts and shiny black shoes—picking off the cream from their tall chocolate parfaits with dainty silver spoons. Donald liked to order cheesecake, which he ate rather messily. "Sex in Japan," he pronounced, his mouth still full of cake, "always seems just around the corner. The invitation is there. One is constantly tempted." And yet, he continued, licking the last crumbs off his lips, "it so often remains just out of reach."

That was not the impression I got from his many seduction stories. A technique he often used, so he once claimed, was to ask a young man on the subway what time the next boat was leaving for Shinagawa. Since Shinagawa was a drab industrial suburb that was once, long ago, the gateway to the city, the question was distinctly odd. But it broke the ice, so to speak, and on occasion might have led to more intimate relations.

But I could see what Donald meant. I had never lived in a

country where the culture of advertising, popular media, and entertainment was as drenched in erotic fantasies as Japan. The pornographic imagination was not furtive and marginal, as in many countries, but entirely upfront. This gave the impression of unlimited sexual possibilities. But a widely shared sense of decorum made sure that this wasn't necessarily so.

And yet the idea of Japan as a sexual paradise for Western men has been around for a very long time, at least in the imagination. Portuguese Jesuits in the late sixteenth century, on a mission to convert the Japanese upper classes, were astonished and not a little shocked by the freedom of women in those days to divorce their husbands, abort unwanted babies, or have extramarital affairs. Chronicles of Japanese life by those early missionaries read like descriptions of the West by strictly orthodox Muslims today. Japanese society has changed a great deal since then. The social freedoms of women, which shocked the Iberian missionaries, became far more constricted in later centuries. But the image of Japan as a licentious place, the country of submissive geisha and Madame Butterflies, persisted.

When the French writer and naval officer known as Pierre Loti came to Japan in 1885, he decided he wanted to marry "a little yellow-skinned woman with black hair and cat's eyes" and live with her in "a little paper house." For a fixed monthly fee of a hundred yen, a temporary match was arranged through an agent who specialized in this kind of thing with a young girl whom Loti immortalized as Madame Chrysanthemum. Incapable of communicating in a common language, or of seeing her as a fully grown human being (she would have been about eighteen), Loti quite literally treated her as if she were a doll, "a mere plaything to laugh at, a little creature of finical forms." This petite doll woman became the model for Madame Butterfly.*

In a way, *Bed and Board*, the movie by François Truffaut that impressed me so much as a student in Leyden, owed something to the same theme. The young Frenchman discarded Kyoko as soon as he got bored playing with her, as Loti had done with Madame Chrysanthemum, and Lieutenant Pinkerton with his Butterfly, as though this were an entirely natural thing to do.

I have already confessed my attraction to Kyoko. Unlike Donald, I did not come to Japan to escape from a society that oppressed my sexual inclinations. And my girlfriend was anything but doll-like. But I cannot imagine wanting to immerse oneself in another culture without feeling a sensual pull. People who study Chinese all their lives without liking Chinese food baffle me. Japan certainly had an erotic frisson for me. As with Max Tessier's love of Japanese cinema, this is not easy to explain. It was not just about the way people look, although that was part of it, but about the peculiar mixture of desire and propriety, abandon and decorum, or what the writer Arthur Koestler once described in a book about Japan as stoic hedonism.

But there was something else, which is hard to express without being accused of racism. In fact, an erotic fixation on another ethnic group cannot be cleanly separated from thinking in racial stereotypes. I once knew an eminent Sinologist, whose knowledge of Chinese civilization matched his love for it. He lived for many years in Beijing. This learned man told me once

---

* Jan van Rij, *Madame Butterfly: Japonisme, Puccini, & the Search for the Real Cho-Cho-San*, Berkeley: Stone Bridge Press, 2001.

that when he made love to a Chinese woman, he couldn't suppress the thought that he was "fucking China."

What he meant, I think, was something close to my fascination with Japanese theater or indeed the Human Pump, an enchantment with the Other, a desire to plumb its mysteries, not just mentally, but physically. The quest is hopeless, of course. You can wake up from an enchantment, but it is in the nature of such mysteries that they elude one's grasp. Perhaps that is what Donald was trying to tell me in the coffee shop. This didn't stop me from trying. There were a number of women; there were one or two men. And there was of course the woman I was living with. But I never did fuck Japan.

Arthur Koestler visited Japan in 1960, after spending some months in India, on a mission to find out whether Asian spirituality had anything to teach people in the West. He was not terribly impressed by what he found, especially in India. In Japan, disgust alternated with euphoria. But his initial impression still sounds right to me: "The first phase of sensuous and sensual delight is the tourist's inevitable reaction to a culture with a surface polish of utterly refined pretty-prettiness, smiling ceremonial, kneeling waitresses, paper-screen houses, dolls, kimonos, and above all, an atmosphere with an erotic flicker like the crisp sparks from a comb drawn through a woman's hair—a guilt-free eroticism which Europe has not known since antiquity."*

In the end, Koestler finds the smiling ceremonial of "this country of stoic hedonists, of Spartan sybarites" irksome, even

---

* *The Lotus and the Robot,* London: Hutchinson, 1960.

robotic. Again, there is the mention of dolls. But there is another way of looking at this. The artificiality of social decorum, the conformity to highly drilled forms of etiquette, can have the paradoxical effect of highlighting what is human and individual. The Kabuki theater, which started in the early seventeenth century as a wild erotic entertainment performed by outcasts, later refined artificiality into the most thrilling dramatic art. Actors actually imitate the movements of Bunraku theater puppets, for which many Kabuki plays were originally conceived. But they are not at all like robots. It is as though the more you press human passions into stylized conventions, the more dramatic they are when they burst into the open.

In the late 1970s, I made a documentary film for Dutch television about the training of young women operating elevators in a department store. There is nothing natural about the behavior of these so-called elevator girls, with their heavily made-up faces, neat uniforms of high-heeled shoes, white gloves, and prim little pillbox hats, their Kabuki-like falsetto voices, and perfectly executed bows at stops on every floor. They not only had many hours of training to distort their natural voices; they had machines to teach them the exact forty-five-degree bow. The effect was uncanny: human beings trimmed like bonsai trees, as mannered as courtiers at the palace of Louis XIV. The intention behind this artfully contrived image of bound femininity, one would like to think, was wholly innocent. But there was also something disturbingly erotic about it, as though the modern department store with its child-like jingles, marble floors, and tinkling elevator music were injected with a hot dash of sadomasochism.

· · ·

IN THE WINTER OF 1976, Sumie and I had decided to split up. My feeling that I was missing out on something in my safe haven no doubt had something to do with this. Erotic paradise beckoned. I wanted to find my way in. And so I moved into a ramshackle apartment on the second floor of an old building in Mejiro, a densely populated area of fine, walled mansions and modest little houses not far from Ikebukuro, one of the railway hubs of Tokyo. The apartment was in the traditional Japanese style, with two rooms, a kitchen, and a bathroom. The main room, which also functioned as a bedroom, had a slightly ratty tatami floor, sliding doors, and wood paneling. The window looked out on a small pond surrounded by bamboo and irises. In the bathroom was an old wooden tub, which tended to get slimy without regular scrubbings, and the toilet was the traditional kind, which meant squatting over a hole.

Such apartments were getting harder to find in Tokyo, where an increasing number of people lived in more modern places with plastic bathtubs, flush toilets, and no tatami mats. My place was a trifle shabby, but I loved it. On the floor below lived an anxious young couple with a small child. They never complained about the floating population that climbed the creaking wooden stairs up to my rooms, where noisy parties were a frequent occurrence.

One of my girlfriends was a jazz singer who belted out Peggy Lee numbers late at night for my benefit—why Peggy Lee, I don't know. Another one was mad about Roxy Music and dressed in black leather trousers. Then there was the student of

French literature who made extra money as a nude dancer in a revue, and talked endlessly about decadent poets in fin de siècle Paris. Another dancer accompanied me on a trip to the rocky Japan Sea coast in midwinter; we made love in tiny run-down wooden inns, while snowflakes tapped the windows like white moths. Of the boys whose acquaintance lasted more than a night, I chiefly remember an art student picked up in a disco, who was always dragging expensive copies of Italian *Vogue* around, which he wished me to translate. I asked him why he didn't buy the American *Vogue,* which would have been a great deal easier. He said he had always dreamed of seeing Rome. I can remember their faces, but alas, most names have faded from my memory. All the while, I was still in touch with Sumie, who lived in our old apartment, unaware of the details of my life but waiting patiently in the serene confidence, as she put it, of Buddha contemplating the monkey dancing on his hand; she was the Buddha, and the monkey, of course, was me.

For several months I shared my apartment with a friend named Rob, who had studied Chinese with me in Leyden. Apart from being a scholar of Chinese literature, he was also a drummer. Soon after his arrival by boat from Taiwan, where he had studied early twentieth century literary chronicles of nightlife in Shanghai, Rob was asked to join a group of aspiring Japanese rock musicians. They were trying to stay afloat by accompanying striptease acts in a seedy entertainment area beyond the city limits. The cabarets in Funabashi had an especially raunchy reputation.

With his gaunt face and shoulder-length blond hair, Rob had a Viking-like air that appealed to Japanese girls whose taste for gaijin matched our own interest in Japanese girls. Rob did not have to ask about the next boat leaving for Shinagawa to attract attention. He did not really have to do anything but smile shyly with a cigarette dangling from his mouth, and girls would come to him, asking whether they might practice their English. Given the right circumstances, the rules of propriety were abandoned with surprising speed. Or perhaps it was more often the case that the foreigner enabled Japanese to dispense with the formal rules. This was one of the perks of being an outsider.

Ethnic or cultural fetishism did not just go one way. One of Rob's conquests, a pretty student named Keiko, was besotted with Eric Clapton. The wall of her tiny room was covered with pictures of Clapton, like a private shrine. She told Rob, on their first meeting in a coffee shop, how much he resembled her idol, which was very far from the truth. He wasn't much bothered by her habit of playing Eric Clapton songs on her cassette tape recorder whenever they had sex. But when she couldn't help herself one day and shouted "Eriku!" into his ear at a moment of supreme passion, even he thought this was carrying things a bit far.

When Rob told me about this encounter, I was reminded of all those specialized coffee shops that cater to musical mono-maniacs, the ones where only opera was played, or free jazz, or rock golden oldies. "Mania" is the word Japanese use for these specialized enthusiasms. Max Tessier had a mania for Japanese cinema. My friend Vassilis had a mania for Mizoguchi's films. Some Japanese girls had a mania for white men, and some for blacks. There was a disco named Mugen, where women trawled for blacks from the various U.S. military bases around Tokyo. Nearby was a pub named Cardinal, popular with young Japanese women looking for gaijin. A female novelist named Yamada Eimi made her name in Japan by writing fiction based on her sexual relations with black men, picked up around U.S. military installations or in discos like Mugen. Her descriptions of dark-skinned sex partners are weirdly similar to Loti's account of his doll woman in Nagasaki, things to play with and then to be discarded.

Yamada's fetish was probably a minority taste. Most Japanese had no interest in intimate relations with gaijin at all; indeed, the very idea might fill them with disgust. But there were clear benefits to being a white male in Japan in the 1970s. Gaijin got more attention than they would ever have received at home, and not just from girls with a Caucasian fetish. The privileges of the outsider were real. It was tempting to confuse rarity with being special, even superior. Already then some Westerners, mostly Americans, were making a good living by appearing on TV as so-called *talento* (talents) even though their only skill was the ability to speak some Japanese. They would pop up on talk shows or variety programs, like trained seals. The studio audience would squeal with delight whenever they opened their mouths. The most famous "gaijin talent," or *gaitare* for short, in the seventies was an American woman who not only spoke Japanese, but did so with a thick Osaka accent.

All this attention could easily lead to undeserved pride. But it was equally tempting to resent one's outsider status and Japanese resistance to the foreigner trying to blend in. I had lunch one day at a Chinese restaurant near the Ginza with an

Australian friend, who went on to have a distinguished career as a playwright. Like me, he had been an early fan of Terayama Shuji's theater. His Japanese was so fluent that he was able to learn the difficult art of Edo Period storytelling, a rare skill even among Japanese. One day he had been invited to show off his proficiency on a well-known television show. I could sense his anger rise as he recalled the occasion. There he was, in the studio, dressed in the traditional kimono worn by premodern storytellers. The television host, a specialist in popular culture, reassured him that he would be treated with great respect, befitting a master of his specialized art. The green light flashed. On he went. Then to his horror, the host roared "Hello!" in English, announced him as the miraculous Japanese-speaking gaijin, and the audience hooted with laughter.

Still flushed at the memory of his humiliation in the television studio, my friend gave our lunch orders to the young waiter standing by our table. The waiter answered in perfectly good English. My friend could no longer contain himself. "Damn it," he said in his fluent Japanese, "why can't you just speak to us in Japanese!" The waiter, a little alarmed by this outburst, confessed that his Japanese was not very good, since he had just arrived from Taiwan.

My own attitude fluctuated, sometimes on the same day, between acceptance, even enjoyment, of my gaijin status, and irritation at being expected to conform to an ethnic type. For most Japanese, a typical gaijin is always white. And not only white, but also American. Asians are never gaijin, and blacks are *kokujin*, meaning blacks. At first, to be asked by curious Japanese whether one could really stomach raw fish, or to be showered with astonished compliments on being able to eat with chopsticks, was OK, even charming. After all, in those days, few Japanese, especially outside the larger cities, had ever met a gaijin in the flesh. Even to be continuously mistaken for an American, and to be quizzed about life in California or New York, was not, on the grander scale of things, an extreme hardship. But after a while it began to grate. One of the few people I knew who had no problem with being a gaijin at all was Donald. He loved "sitting on [his] perch, unassailable, observing the world from a distance."

What is sure is that many Japanese vastly preferred a foreigner to behave according to type than to act like a Japanese. Not long after I moved into my apartment in Mejiro, I was asked by an American photographer named Greg to go down to Kyoto with him, where he had arranged to take pictures in a venerable old geisha house. Greg, a large disheveled Vietnam vet, needed me to interpret, since he didn't speak any Japanese.

Kyoto geisha houses are very traditional establishments, with their own strict rules of etiquette, as elaborate as those of a royal court. I was determined to be on my best Japanese behavior, bowing in the proper manner, and using the polite Japanese phrases expressing our relative status. I took off my shoes and entered the house, bowing low and voicing the customary apologies to the proprietress as she slid open the lovely paper doors ("We are so sorry to bother you at such a busy time," and so on). She bowed back, but couldn't quite conceal a look of bewilderment, as though I was slightly mad. I then heard Greg clatter onto the wooden floor, a wide grin on his face, shouting

"Hey, mama-san!" A look of boundless relief lit up the face of the dainty-looking lady in her expensive kimono. "Hi, Greg-san. How are you?" she replied in Kyoto-accented English.

But, of course, television studios and geisha houses are not representative of Japanese society. One's personal friends did not treat a foreigner as though he were a trained seal. Nogami-san, Kurosawa's oldest assistant, and producer of the Suntory whiskey commercials, was such a friend, an elegant cosmopolitan woman at ease with people wherever they came from. After my appearance with Max Tessier in the commercial shoot at Kurosawa's country house, she asked me once more to be in a Suntory ad, this time without the great director. I was to be an extra in a bar scene, drinking whiskey with a number of other gaijin. My flatmate Rob was included in the invitation.

Rob and I were told where to stand on the set inside the Toho studio, where so many of Kurosawa's masterpieces had been made. There was a long American-style wooden bar, and a barman brandishing cocktail shakers like maracas. Our fellow extras were mostly recruited from a nearby U.S. military base. They included a number of black marines. The director, no longer intimidated by Kurosawa's imperious presence, was strutting about like a maestro, giving loud instructions to his cameraman and sound crew. Lights were adjusted. And the director, a thin man with dark glasses and a white cotton hat, the requisite look of a Japanese moviemaker, called for action.

We chatted with the marines in what we thought was an animated fashion and sipped from our glasses filled with whiskey-colored barley tea. "Cut, cut!" shouted the director in a state of great agitation. We wondered what we had done wrong, but were perfectly willing to start again. "Action!" Once more we talked, a bit louder this time, and drank our tea. "Cut!" shouted the director. "No, no, no," he said. "Let me show you." He walked up to where the black marines were standing, and started waving his arms about wildly, like an angry gorilla. "Like this," he explained, jabbing the air with his fists, "more like blacks!"

The marines began to laugh. "Oh, OK," they said, "we get it." And after the director had called for action once more, the black men started hopping around, yelling and high-fiving, like basketball players after a slam dunk. This time, the director made the thumbs-up sign. He was happy. The guys did not seem to be offended at all. They were old hands at this.

THAT ETHNIC FANTASIES did not just run from East to West and vice versa became clear to me one memorable afternoon at the Film Center in Kyobashi. One movie that left a deeper impression on me than many great films I had seen was by no means a masterpiece. It was shown as part of a series of Japanese wartime pictures. Directed by a studio hack named Fushimizu Osamu, *Shina no Yoru* (*China Nights*) was shot in 1940 on location in Shanghai, then under Japanese military occupation, and at the very Toho studio where I had appeared as an extra in the whiskey commercial. The two main stars were Hasegawa Kazuo, a heartthrob whose famous profile was slashed with a razor by a gangster hired by his studio when the actor decided to move to a rival company, and a petite young actress named Li Xianglan from Manchukuo, then a Japanese puppet state in what used to be called Manchuria and is now northeastern China.

Hasegawa is an officer in the Japanese merchant navy. Walking along the waterfront in Shanghai one day, he sees several Japanese thugs accost a young Chinese woman (Li). He rescues the woman and puts her up in his hostel called the Yamato House (Yamato being an old patriotic name for Japan). Li, who lost both her parents in the war with Japan, fiercely resists the good-hearted attentions of her benefactor and his kind Japanese friends. Her obstinacy drives Hasegawa into such a rage that he slaps her face. Japanese audiences at the time interpreted this notorious slap as a sincere token of his passion for her. Chinese saw it as an affront and loathed Li for humiliating the entire nation by lending herself to this despicable scene. In the end, the merchant seaman manages to win her over. She falls in love with him and at last recognizes the benevolent intentions of the Japanese.

They decide to get married. But before the happy Sino-Japanese union can take place, Hasegawa's ship is ambushed by Chinese "bandits," as Japanese called all partisans. A gun battle ensues. Convinced that her lover is dead and frantic with grief, Li goes to the place of the ambush, a beautiful spot with a lovely pagoda overlooking an ancient canal. She sings a Japanese children's song (one of the curiosities of *China Nights* is that the Chinese girl starts to speak in flawless Japanese about halfway through the movie), and wades into the picturesque canal fully intending to die. Then a miracle happens: the Japanese seaman turns out to be alive. He hears her song, lifts her out of the water, and the lovers embrace in silhouette, the moving symbol of Sino-Japanese solidarity in the war against Western imperialism.

This, at any rate, was the ending shown in cinemas in China, where the mawkish sentiments convinced no one. An alternative scene was shot especially for Japanese audiences, in which the heroine does indeed die by drowning herself in the canal, thus conforming to the romantic Japanese stereotype of the woman sacrificing herself for the love of her man.

The movie is remarkable enough as a piece of propaganda. Even more famous than the film was the lilting theme song, warbled by Li Xianglan herself: *"China nights, ah, China nights / a lantern softly swinging outside the willow window / a red bird cage / China girl singing love songs / sad love songs . . ."* The melody is a pastiche of Chinese music, a piece of chinoiserie for Japanese consumption. Li Xianglan, or Ri Koran in Japanese pronunciation, may have been excoriated for her treachery in China, but she became enormously popular in Japan, setting off a kind of boom in Chinese music and fashion. Japanese girls wanted to look like Ri Koran. People queued around the block to hear her sing at the biggest concert hall in Tokyo. And this was in 1940, when the war in China was raging. Only three years before *China Nights*, the Imperial Japanese Army had murdered and raped possibly hundreds of thousands of civilians in the Chinese capital of Nanjing.

The main reason for Li's, or Ri's, popularity was not her acting ability, which was modest, or her singing, which was only a little better, but her exotic appearance, exotic in Japanese eyes. A small woman with large swimming eyes, a lotus flower stuck in her hair, always dressed in silk Chinese robes, Ri was not a conventional beauty. But to Japanese in the 1940s she represented continental glamour. She was the face of pan-Asian propaganda, of all the "yellow-skinned races" happy to submit to the beneficent power of the Japanese Empire. In short, Ri Koran was an erotic fantasy.

If the movie itself was memorable, the story behind it was even more so. For Li Xianglan was not really Chinese at all. Her actual name was Yamaguchi Yoshiko, a Japanese born in Manchuria in 1920. Her father, a chancer looking for adventure on the continent, taught Chinese to Japanese employees of the South Manchurian Railway Company. He was also a gambler, and financial trouble forced him to ask a sympathetic Chinese general to adopt his daughter. Perfectly bilingual in Japanese and Chinese, Yoshiko acquired some Russian, too, from her voice teacher, a White Russian opera singer who had fled to Manchuria after the revolution.

In the late 1930s, the Manchukuo Film Association, run entirely by Japanese and financed by the Japanese army, was looking for a Chinese actress to perform in propaganda pictures as the local girl who falls in love with brave Japanese soldiers or engineers, thus promoting the Japanese cause. It proved to be impossible to find a Chinese actress who was either willing or able to fit the bill. After more casting around, the studio boss heard a young singer on the Manchukuo radio singing in three languages. The lure of stardom sufficed to persuade the girl to do her patriotic duty. And so the young Yoshiko was swiftly transformed into a Chinese actress, named Li Xianglan. Her true identity remained a closely guarded state secret.

After the Japanese defeat in 1945, Chinese patriots in Shanghai arrested her as a traitor. The only way she could save herself from certain execution was to prove who she was by producing the necessary Japanese documents. Luckily for her, she had a powerful protector who was more than a father figure to her, the Japanese movie producer Kawakita Nagamasa, the man I sometimes saw hovering around the corridors of the Film Center in Tokyo. Yamaguchi Yoshiko, as she became once more, was his mistress for a time. Donald Richie remembered seeing her breaking down in loud sobs at the funeral of Kashiko, Kawakita's wife. "Mother! Mother!" she cried, perhaps a little too histrionically, as the woman she had cuckolded was being laid to her eternal rest.

Yamaguchi's career picked up again under the U.S. occupation. American intelligence officers knew all about her, because *China Nights* was one of the films most frequently used for their Japanese language instruction. The pseudo-Chinese theme song had become famous in OSS training centers. Renamed Shirley Yamaguchi, the actress soon appeared in Hollywood films, such as *House of Bamboo* (1955), starring Robert Ryan as an American gangster in occupied Tokyo. The movie poster shows her half naked, the perfect "geisha girl" in the male American imagination. In one notable scene, she softly massages the naked back of Robert Stack, while murmuring that "Japanese women are born to please their men."

I was deeply struck by this double, or triple performance act, the Japanese woman pretending to be Chinese, acting in Japanese movies, the exotic pan-Asian and sultry geisha girl, the star who invited Japanese men to imagine fucking China, and Americans to fuck Japan.

Yamaguchi's bizarre story reminded me in a peculiar way

of my own childhood. From an early age I was used to seeing cultural behavior as a kind of performance. With my maternal grandparents, themselves ultra-English children of German-Jewish immigrants, I acted the role of the perfect English boy, and reverted to being Dutch at home in The Hague, where I spent my early childhood playing cricket with Dutch Anglophiles putting on English airs, for entirely snobbish reasons, to set them apart from Dutch hoi polloi, just as a few generations before the smart set had spoken French in a lingering echo of aristocratic affectation. I fetishized Englishness long before I ever thought of Japan. Ri Koran spoke to me as a symbol, not so much of pan-Asianism, which obviously meant nothing to me, as of the ways we let our fantasies roam across national and racial borderlines, and of life as a continuing act.

About ten years after seeing *China Nights,* I met Yamaguchi Yoshiko. She was a minister of parliament for the conservative Liberal Democratic Party. Hoping to improve relations with China, the party had recruited her as a kind of cultural diplomat. This was after she had reinvented herself once more, in the 1960s, as a television host, specializing in exclusive interviews with third-world dictators, such as Idi Amin and Kim Il-sung. The Palestinian cause, too, was one of her concerns, which brought her into the orbit of radical fringe groups on the far left, including some of the fellow travelers of the Japanese Red Army who had become directors of porno films.

She spoke to me in a mixture of Chinese and Japanese, sometimes switching in midsentence. I can't imagine that she would have done this when speaking to a Japanese. But I represented the outside world. We were sitting in her office near the Diet building. She still looked very much like a former movie star: not a wrinkle on her soft chalk-white face, large purple-framed spectacles, and jet-black hair with a lacquer-like sheen. An assistant in fluffy slippers poured us cups of green tea.

"I still feel that China is my home," she said. "I now look back at those films with shame. But I was young and did as I was told. I didn't think I was doing anything wrong. You see, I saw myself as a bridge of friendship between Japan and the country of my birth." Her eyes opened wide, in the helpless way I remembered from *China Nights* when she declared her love for the Japanese sailor, or in the way Princess Diana used to gain the sympathy of male journalists. I felt as if I was witnessing another well-practiced piece of theater.

I asked her about meeting Idi Amin, Saddam Hussein, Mao Zedong, Yasser Arafat, and Kim Il-sung. "Ah, Kim Il-sung," she said softly, "a much misunderstood man. He had the warmest handshake, and such piercing eyes. It was as if he could see straight through you." And Chairman Mao . . . She appeared for a moment to be overcome with emotion. A light tremor went through her frame. "He was a great man, a great Asian man. And do you know what he said to me? He said that he had seen *China Nights* during the war and he thanked me for it. I felt as though a great weight had been lifted off my shoulders."

I didn't quite know what to say. A better interviewer might have pushed her more. After a moment's silence, she said: "I know I was once on the wrong side of things. That is why I want us all to be friends. I will be a bridge between peoples. That is my goal, my life's work."

China Nights continued to haunt me through the years. I

met Yamaguchi a few times afterward, but she remained an enigma. All I ever got was a repeat performance. Her story had become a modern myth in Japan, celebrated in several movies, more than one ghosted autobiography, a play, a musical, and even a number of manga. She was never going to depart from the myth. I ended up writing a novel about her many years later, which is less a story about her actual life, the truth of which remains elusive, than a fictional account of her invented one.

IN THE END, I had to leave my beloved apartment in Mejiro. The owners, a businessman with a crooked row of shiny gold teeth and his dreadful beady-eyed wife, wanted to tear the building down and build a modern apartment block, or perhaps a car park. I didn't want to move, and neither did the anxious couple living downstairs. It is difficult to kick sitting tenants out in Japan, as long as they pay their rent in escrow at the local ward office. At first, the wife would drop by in an attempt to persuade us to move. I told her that I couldn't afford to right now. Her eyes narrowed and a shrewd little smile cracked her powdery face: "We all know what gaijin are like. We know you gaijin are good at making money."

Always alert to an anti-Semitic slur, I thought of all the books I had seen at various stores in Tokyo explaining how Jews really ran the world. But I don't think that is what she meant. Gaijin probably just meant gaijin: greedy, materialistic, crude.

Persuasion soon changed to pressure. The anxious young mother downstairs was in tears one day after the landlady had threatened her, and warned that the house would collapse in an earthquake and her child would surely die. The landlady then threatened to alert my university if I continued to refuse to comply with her wishes. And sure enough, I was soon summoned to the office of the president of the arts school, a smiling bureaucrat who told me that he had heard about a certain problem to do with housing. I should of course understand that the university should never be inconvenienced in this manner again.

And so I moved to a one-room apartment in an old geisha district, next door to a couple of fervent believers in the Soka Gakkai Buddhist movement. They would leave a copy of their religious paper at my door every day, until the pile of unread journals became too high and had to be removed. I used my tiny lavatory as an improvised darkroom to develop film. Next door was an old-fashioned public bathhouse, where I would go for a wash every evening. My fellow bathers were very polite. They pretended that I wasn't there.

TO CLAIM THAT what happened later had anything to do with my odious landlady in Mejiro, or the pusillanimity of the Nichidai arts school president, would be disingenuous. There is simply no excuse for it. My behavior on New Year's Eve in Kyoto was simply disgraceful.

Five of us traveled down to Kyoto: my friend Tsuda, my flatmate Rob, an American student of Japanese history named Jim, a fellow Nichidai student we called Kin-san, and myself. Junko, a young avant-garde dancer who had attached herself to Rob, joined us later. We all stayed in one room at a rather dilapidated inn on the Kamo River. The inn, like similar places in the neighborhood, had once been a brothel. After prostitution was officially banned in the late 1950s, many of these old houses were converted into cheap inns, catering mostly to young foreigners. Japanese tended to stay away from them, worried about their disreputable associations. The kind old lady who ran the inn, named O-Kinu, had herself once worked there as a prostitute. She had fond memories of American soldiers during the postwar occupation.

The first day of the year is the most important festive day in Japan. Families gather to eat sumptuous cold delicacies all day, carefully prepared long before the event. Friends are invited to drink sake and eat sticky rice balls in miso broth from the early morning, usually after visiting temples and shrines the night before. O-Kinu, who might have been a prostitute but was a proud stickler for Kyoto tradition, promised that we would wake up to a spread of Kyoto New Year dishes in the morning.

Tsuda had also arranged something special for New Year's Day. He had always been good at making an impression on old ladies, who saw him as a promising intellectual whom they could help on his way to an illustrious literary career. One of these ladies was a very refined person from an old Kyoto family. She lived in a beautiful traditional house with a well-kept Japanese garden, and a room for tea ceremonies. She had kindly invited Tsuda to bring his friends for a traditional New Year's lunch.

We didn't give much thought to all these feasts to come, as we set out on the frosty New Year's Eve, with the stars blazing brightly over the snow-covered temple roofs of Kyoto. The streets were filled with throngs of young Japanese, many of them dressed in kimonos for the occasion, slowly shuffling their way to the ancient religious places that had miraculously survived the war, since at the last minute Kyoto had been struck off the list of cities to be obliterated by an atom bomb. (The story goes that Secretary of War Henry L. Stimson had visited Kyoto before the war and couldn't bear the idea of destroying this historic city.)

We had already drunk quite a lot of beer, and were now passing around a huge bottle of sake, which we drank straight from the bottle. Dizzy from drink and the freezing cold, we began to get a little boisterous. There would be no chance that these gaijin were going to be politely ignored this time. I cannot remember whether it was Jim or myself who decided that it would be a splendid joke to reverse roles and subject Japanese strangers to all the clichés that we had had to hear in our daily lives. Can you stomach raw fish? we would ask astonished passersby. What about chopsticks? How amazing that you can use them so skillfully. And could you tell us all about America? And so it went on, as we got steadily more inebriated and obnoxious. In any other country we would have received a fully justified thrashing. We can only thank Japanese politeness for the fact that we did not.

Tsuda and Kin-san pretended to find all of this highly entertaining as well. One large bottle of sake followed another. After midnight, I literally could not stand on my feet any longer and had to be dragged back to our inn, where Kin-san fell straight through the glass window of our room, creating a cold draft that none of us noticed since we swiftly fell into a deep sleep, except for Jim, or Rob, and the young dancer. One of them, or perhaps both—no one could quite recall—had had sex with the dancer on the matted floor in the midst of shards of glass.

We woke up late the next morning to find the beautifully prepared dishes laid out by O-Kinu on the table, with little bottles of sake for each of us. Just looking at food or drink was enough to make us feel sick. Rob and Kin-san rolled over moaning and fell into a kind of coma. When O-Kinu came in to wish us a happy New Year and ask whether we had enjoyed the meal, I had to make excuses and explain that we had had a rough night. Her eyes took in the scene of utter pandemonium in the room and she withdrew without saying a word.

It was about two in the afternoon when we finally roused ourselves with pounding headaches and queasy stomachs to visit Tsuda's kind and elegant patroness. We had been expected at noon. The square black table was covered in the daintiest dishes, beautifully prepared herring roe and chrysanthemum-shaped lotus roots in black lacquer boxes, plump red salmon roe and giant grilled shrimp brined in sugar. Our hostess, dressed in a graceful kimono of discreet pink and gray flower patterns, explained, without a hint of annoyance, that it would have been so much better if we had arrived on time, since the colors of the bowls and plates had been especially chosen to match the light shining through the rice-paper windows. As it was later now, she had been forced replace the utensils with a different set to match the time of day.

As she was explaining this, and we were trying to pick at some of the dishes for the sake of politeness, Tsuda had withdrawn to the lavatory, emitting awful gurgling noises, which we were all studiously pretending not to hear. Despite our delicate physical condition, we managed to sit through the lunch making polite conversation. Jim picked up one of the lovely tea bowls, turned it around, and asked if it was from the Edo Period. Yes, said the kind lady, "you are quite right. You foreigners are so knowledgeable. We Japanese are quite ignorant in comparison. But it isn't quite from the Edo Period, but a little bit older than that. Azuchi Momoyama, actually, late sixteenth century."

After Tsuda had finally emerged from his ablutions, it was almost time to leave. The sun was already sinking, casting a lovely glow onto the exquisite dishes we had left largely untouched on the table. We thanked our hostess profusely and apologized for having been late. "Never mind," said the lady. "You are all most welcome to come back at any time."

I was the first to climb down from the wooden hallway into the stone entrance where our shoes were waiting for us in a perfect straight line. I bent over my shoes, about to put them on, facing the door, with my back to my friends and the lady of the house who was bowing them out. And out it came, I could not help it, like a short blast from a trumpet. There was a second of stunned silence. I stood up. We all pretended that we hadn't heard or smelled a thing.

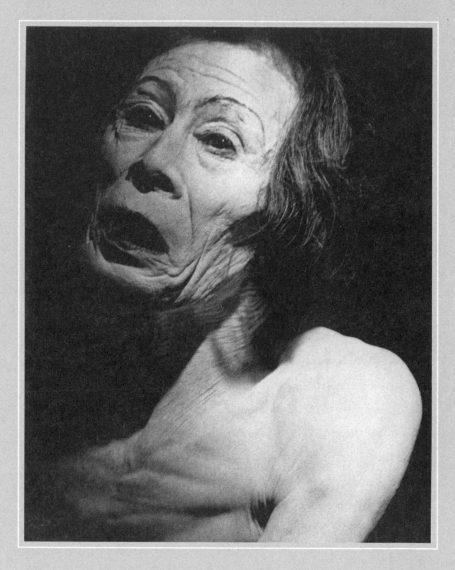

Ono Kazuo dancing in his seventies

SIX

New Year's Eve, 1977, at the Asbestos Studio. This two-story building in Meguro Ward was named after the poisonous insulation material manufactured there before it became a dance studio. Various people on the ground floor were taking turns pounding sticky rice with a heavy wooden mallet to produce traditional rice cakes for the New Year. I knew that many of them were famous. But I recognized only a few, and had little idea of how distinguished they actually were: Ikeda Masuo, the print artist and novelist, thin like a dandelion, with bushy curls sprouting from his narrow head, was sprawled on the floor fast asleep, despite the hubbub around him. Japan's greatest modern poet, Tanikawa Shuntaro, was in deep conversation with Shibusawa Tatsuhiko, the pale-skinned essayist and translator of the Marquis de Sade. Shibusawa wore dark glasses and spoke formal eighteenth-century French in a soft halting voice. Hosoe Eikoh, the photographer, who once took pictures of Mishima posing naked as Saint Sebastian, pierced by arrows, pointed his camera at a group of male dancers with shaven heads like brown eggs, bobbing up and down in the melee. I noticed the architect Isozaki Arata, and Ono Kazuo, a refined-looking gentleman in his seventies, who was well known for his slow stylized tango dance performances in white-lace ball gowns, performances he would continue into his nineties, even though he could barely walk. Shiraishi Kazuko, the sexy poet and former lover of Muhammad Ali, was there. Yamashita Yosuke, the free-jazz pianist in steel-rimmed glasses, was pouring sake for Maro Akaji, an actor and a dancer.

I was tagging along with Maro. Come and meet Hijikata-san, he said. I knew who Hijikata was, of course. Everyone interested in theater and dance in Japan did. He was the father of Ankoku Butoh, or Dance of Darkness, the modern Japanese dance form more or less invented by Hijikata in the late 1950s as a deliberately grotesque aesthetic reaction against Western ballet and classical Japanese dance. Hijikata had just given up dancing himself, but as a choreographer he was still king of the Butoh world. The Asbestos Studio was his company. His father-in-law had owned the old asbestos factory. I had first seen Hijikata at a performance by Maro Akaji's troupe. "There he is, there he is," people around me whispered, as he passed by our seats with his chief dancer, Ashikawa Yoko. A tall man, with a wispy beard, thick black eyebrows, and long salt-and-pepper hair tied loosely in a knot, he looked like a guru of some sort, pretending to ignore the commotion his entrance had caused.

I protested that I would have nothing to say to the great man. No, Maro insisted, I should be properly introduced. We went up the narrow stairs to a big loft-like space, where Hijikata was sitting at a long wooden table, talking to a number of

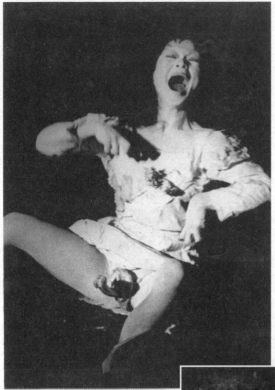

Dancers in
Hijikata Tatsumi's
Asbestos Studio

people, most of whom I didn't recognize. Ashikawa sat next to him, a fine-boned woman with small myopic eyes and a prominent jaw. Onstage, grimacing in white face, her eyes almost disappearing into their sockets, her blackened teeth bared, she looked like the decaying corpse of one of those stylized Kabuki actors in an eighteenth-century print.

Hijikata told his star dancer to move up and patted the cushion next to him, telling me to sit down. Maro introduced me as a young film student who knew Donald Richie. Hijikata nodded politely. He had known Donald since 1959, when Hijikata gave his first Butoh performance, inspired by Mishima's novel *Forbidden Colors*, about the seduction of a beautiful young man by a cynical old novelist. The show, in which a priapic Hijikata acted out the rape of the young man, danced by Ono Kazuo's son with a live chicken squeezed between his thighs, had caused an uproar in Tokyo. Donald had come to see it with Mishima. He was so impressed that he decided to make a film with the dancer.

Donald's ten-minute film, called *Sacrifice,* shot with an 8mm camera, was long thought to have been lost, but was found and restored to its original, slightly underexposed condition. To the sound of Handel's *Messiah,* a young dancer is assaulted by a group of delirious men and women in flapping kimonos, who shit and vomit all over him before castrating him with a meat cleaver.

I had not seen the movie when I met Hijikata, nor do I recall whether I had even heard of it then. But I knew that Hijikata's work was suffused with pain, torture, and death. He talked a great deal about Jean Genet. His favorite artist was Hans Bell-

mer, the German surrealist in Paris who specialized in mutilated female dolls and fine drawings of erotic perversities.
Hijikata based several of his dance pieces on works by de Sade.

"So, young man," he said, kindly pouring a cup of sake for
me, "what exactly do you do?" I explained that I was studying
cinema. He grunted. "Studying, studying, we're all studying,
but what are you intending to do with your studies?" I mumbled something about photography and film, but without much
conviction.

"What was your name again?" I told him my name, Buruma, which in Japanese sounds more like "bloomers," pronounced "Buroomah." "Ah," he said. "Underpants. So, my dear
pants, what music do you like? Tell me something unusual,
something I don't know." Too intimidated to answer, I asked
him what his favorite music was. "Why change the subject?" he
asked. "We were talking about you."

I could sense that I was boring him. He then decided to put
on a little show, not for my benefit, but more in a fit of drunken
lassitude, to change the mood. "Ashikawa!" he barked at his
chief dancer. "Go out and buy some more sake." She looked
perplexed. "But, Sensei," she muttered, "it's past midnight. The
shops are closed." It was hard to tell whether Hijikata was really angry, or whether it was just for display. "Didn't you hear
what I said? Go out and bring me more sake!" He waved his
hand dismissively. "Go, go, go!"

And off she went, also for show, hanging around in the freezing night until she felt that it was OK to come back and tell the
master that she had tried her best. In the meantime, Hijikata
had given up on me, and talked rather interestingly about Hans

Bellmer. His dolls of women in all kinds of grotesque contortions, made in the 1930s, were a protest against the Nazi cult of healthy Aryan bodies. Bellmer's dolls bore a resemblance to Butoh dancers and their tortured movements. Japanese bodies, Hijikata explained, were not like long-limbed gaijin bodies: "All our power is in the thighs. So we don't stretch when we dance, we squat, we like to get close to the earth." This remark came back to me much later when I finally saw Donald's film *Sacrifice,* when a woman slowly sinks her body over the sacrificial victim and pisses on him before she helps to slice off his balls.

Hijikata then switched the topic to Abe Sada, the prostitute who cut off her lover's penis after strangling him in an erotic game, the subject of *In the Realm of the Senses.* "I knew Sada," said Hijikata. "She was an artist. Artists must be like criminals. They must draw blood."

While the sensei spoke, everyone around the table kept quiet, nodding at his aperçus. Silently, Ashikawa slipped back into the room. Hijikata didn't even ask her whether she had managed to procure any sake. Perhaps he had forgotten all about it. "Pants," he said, as I made to go back downstairs. "You know what you are? You're a television."

I'm still not entirely sure what he meant, but I think I know. He had not meant it kindly, but he had a point. I was still soaking up the lives of others, studying instead of creating anything, reflecting back, like a camera, rather than giving anything of myself. But I had been offered the chance, in a minor way, to do so. In the year leading up to New Year's Eve at the Asbestos Studio I had begun to dip one foot at least into the dance world myself.

SOMETIME IN THE SPRING OF 1977, Ritsaert ten Cate turned up in Tokyo. I had seen him before in Amsterdam but never really got to know him. He was the founder of the Mickery Theater, where I had first seen Terayama's Tenjo Sajiki. The son of a wealthy textile manufacturer, Ritsaert was extraordinary to look at, especially in Tokyo. Very tall, clumsy in his movements, with a booming voice, he had a face like an unmade bed: hooded eyes, loose cheeks, lips like two cuts of liver, and long strands of blond hair streaming from the back of a large bald head. In moments of boredom, he was given to putting on silly Dutch voices, which must have baffled the Japanese.

Maro Akaji

119

Ritsaert was also one of the most important international theater impresarios of the twentieth century. He nurtured the talents of Peter Sellars, Willem Dafoe, Robert Wilson, and many others. And the Japanese knew it, so he was treated with great deference.

Ritsaert had come to find out what was going on in the Japanese theater. And I was to be his guide. We buzzed around town in a yellow Fiat, driven by a long-haired photographer named "Herbie" Yamaguchi, who was the boyfriend of Terayama's ex-wife, a chain-smoking former show dancer, to whom I gave weekly English lessons. Her stage name was Kujo Eiko. She managed the Tenjo Sajiki.

Despite his shambling appearance, Ritsaert was a deeply cultivated man with an instinctive feel for the theater. "I don't judge art with my head," he liked to say, "I have to feel it in my balls." He had heard about Hijikata and his Butoh dancers from Kujo, and seen some film footage. His aim, fruitless as it turned out, was to coax Hijikata into performing in Amsterdam. The main Butoh troupe in Tokyo, aside from the Asbestos Studio, was Maro Akaji's Dairakudakan. Ritsaert wanted to meet Maro too.

Maro agreed to see us at the Dairakudakan studio in a crowded residential area in the southeast of Tokyo. He looked as remarkable as Ritsaert. With a clean-shaven head, a black moustache drooping down the sides of his mouth, and observant hangdog eyes, there was something melancholy and also faintly sinister about him. In fact, he was warm and humorous. But I could see why Kara Juro used to cast him as lugubrious ghosts and other grotesques, when Maro had been one of the main actors in Kara's Situation Theater in the 1960s. I could also see why Maro appeared in many movies as a monster of one kind or another.

Both Kara and Maro regarded Hijikata as their theatrical mentor. He had taught them to use the body as the central element in drama. Hijikata, and after him others in the avant-garde theater, rebelled against the academic style of theater in Japan. Too often, in the recent past, Japanese actors and dancers appeared to be mimicking Westerners. The way back to authenticity, as it were, was not to revive Japanese traditions, such as Noh or Kabuki, which had already become theatrical museum pieces, but to revive the spirit of Japanese drama, expressed through a stylized, sometimes violent use of the body. Terayama encouraged his actors to confront the audience physically. Kara's actors used their bodies in the exaggerated manner of slapstick comedians. Maro left Kara's group in the early 1970s to form the Dairakudakan, the most theatrical of the Butoh companies. Maro is not a trained dancer, but an actor who uses body language instead of words to perform his deliberately outlandish dance theater pieces. Kara and Terayama stuck with words. Maro abandoned them.

Ritsaert and I sat on the wooden floor of Maro's studio, watching his dancers moving like embalmed corpses slowly coming to life, limbs twitching, faces grimacing, eyes rolling, mouths opened wide in silent screams. They crawled and slithered, they squatted and twisted their bodies like those Bellmer dolls. Since this was a rehearsal, they did not wear the full-body Butoh makeup of white rice flour. But the men were all as hairless as Buddhist monks. Some had even shaved off their eyebrows. The loud metallic sound of Tangerine Dream, the German rock group, was jangling on a tape recorder.

I asked Ritsaert what he thought, after we got back to his hotel. He shrugged his shoulders. He couldn't explain why he wasn't all that impressed. Hijikata was the real thing, he kept repeating. I couldn't understand his skepticism. I thought the dancers were extraordinary. It was only later, long after he had returned to Amsterdam, that I grasped what Ritsaert knew instinctively. What we had seen at Maro's rehearsal studio was a very Japanese phenomenon. A theatrical method that had been created by a great artist, through sheer daring and experimentation, had become established as a style, passed on by masters of various schools, all with their own variations. This had happened to the tea ceremony, once a spontaneous expression of aesthetic joy in drinking tea, now a rigid set of rules, to be learned by wealthy ladies who pay a fortune to the various tea ceremony schools. The same thing had happened to classical theater and to flower arranging. And now, in a way, it was happening even to a once avant-garde dance form.

This didn't mean that Maro's group was mediocre. He was an extraordinary performer and his dancers were superb. Nor was he simply imitating his master. What was lacking was the danger of Hijikata's early work, when anything could happen, and people could still be outraged. This was not just a matter of personalities. Much of what was developed in the 1960s became formalized, even mannered in later years. Terayama Shuji died in 1983. His acolytes still perform his plays in the style that he laid down; his theatrical innovations gelled into a set of patterns, as inflexible in their ways as the ritualized moves in Kabuki or Noh. This is not a uniquely Japanese phenomenon. But it is perhaps more pronounced in Japan.

I was drawn to Butoh from the first time I saw it. Though highly sophisticated, it was yet another variation of the erotic, grotesque, absurd strain in Japanese culture, an avant-garde expression of *nostalgie de la boue*. My own interest in this doubtless sprang from a different source than Hijikata's, who was born in the muddy rice lands of northeastern Japan. I was in any case ready to prove that I was more than a television camera looking from the outside in. As it happened, this coincided with a common desire among Japanese artists to reach out to the world outside their native archipelago.

Unlike Hijikata, Maro was keen to take his company abroad. The Dance of Darkness had already spawned a number of groups in Japan, led by amazing personalities bearing odd stage names. "Bishop" Yamada once appeared in Maro's studio with two young nude dancers on a leash crawling ahead of him like prized dogs. There was a lot of talk in the studio of spreading Butoh all over the world, like a movement that would grow and grow. The idea of half-naked Japanese dancers covered in white rice flour, twisting their bodies in a simulation of life after death, sweeping the world seemed preposterous to me. But I was wrong. Since the 1980s, Butoh troupes have performed in many parts of Europe and the United States, as well as Asia. The best-known group outside Japan is probably Amagatsu Ushio's Sankai Juku, which has performed in more than sixty countries. In 1985, one of the dancers, suspended by his ankles on a rope dangling from the sixth floor of the Mutual Life Building in Seattle, fell to his death when the rope snapped. It was a frightful accident, of course. But the dancer never changed his rigid position, as though sticking to his performance as he plunged. The fatal act was called *Dance of Birth and Death.*

Amagatsu was one of Maro's main dancers when I began to visit the studio regularly. Born in 1949, he was six years younger than Maro. Hijikata was born in 1928, Mishima in 1925, Terayama in 1935, Kara Juro in 1940. There were rumors that Hijikata had trained to be a kamikaze pilot, but was saved at the last minute from suicidal death by Japan's surrender. Terayama lost his father in the war and barely escaped from the bombing of his hometown. Kara was evacuated from Tokyo as a child, and came back to find nothing but devastation. Maro's mother went insane after her husband was killed in the war. Amagatsu grew up in Yokosuka, a rough town that was once the main base of the Imperial Japanese Navy and was taken over in 1945 by the U.S. Navy. All these artists, in one way or another, were marked by the war and its aftermath. They grew up with horrific violence, or its wreckage. Mishima, a frail and bookish young man, was declared unfit for military service and regretted it forever. All he could do was act out brutal and heroic fantasies in his novels, as a film actor and a photographic model, and finally, for real, in the bloody coup de théâtre of his public samurai suicide.

Death and rebirth are the main themes of the Dance of Darkness. Every piece directed for the Dairakudakan by Maro revolved around it. It was as though this form of dance theater reflected the painful rebirth of Japan from the ashes of the catastrophe it had unleashed. Butoh was not only a reaction to prissy Western and Japanese high culture; it was also the expression of several generations of Japanese who had lived with violent death. Hence, the mummified bodies in white makeup, twisted and contorted like corpses after a bombing raid, creeping back toward life.

Despite the morbidity of their art, Maro and his troupe were enormous fun to be with. We would talk through the night about dance, culture, sex, and literature, while consuming huge amounts of alcohol. The one thing we didn't do was drugs. In the chaos of the occupation years, many Japanese used a methamphetamine called *hiropon,* providing a tidy income for gangsters. Some rock and rollers took other kinds of speed pills. And young people could be seen slumped against the walls of underground shopping malls or railway stations sniffing glue from plastic bags. But even among "underground" theater folks, there was very little use of cannabis or cocaine. A famous female pop singer was caught once with some marijuana. She had to offer a public apology and was banned from the major television shows.

Maro insisted that I train together with his dancers. It was no good just to be a watcher; I had to put my body into it if I wanted to understand what they were doing. And so I, too, wriggled and contorted and squatted, even though my dancing skills were minimal. But that didn't seem to bother Maro. "Skill isn't the point," he said. "I want to know what you're made of." He would make me stand still on the studio floor and study me through rings of cigarette smoke, a bit like a palm reader scrutinizing the lines of a person's hand. "Each body has a spirit," he would say, "an aura." I felt more comfortable dancing badly than having my aura examined in this manner. Maro took another puff of his cigarette, and just laughed.

Since the contemporary arts in Japan receive no official subsidies, Butoh dancers were sent out to cabarets and strip shows to generate extra income for their groups. Hijikata started this practice. Maro, as well as Kara and his Korean-Japanese wife, Ri Reisen, used to perform something called "the kinpun show." Their naked bodies—naked apart from a tiny piece of cloth covering the genitals, like a skimpy jockstrap—were painted gold, like the girl in the James Bond movie *Goldfinger.* They would dance in smoky little clubs on the outskirts of Tokyo to the music of Tom Jones or Barry Manilow on scratchy tapes, or sometimes in the better clubs to live bands.

One day Maro announced that it was my turn to do a show. I protested that I wasn't ready for it. Maro grinned, and said that all I had to do was to stand still, strike a pose, and let the girl do the dancing around me. My partners would be a couple, who went by the name of Dance Love Machine. They were excellent dancers, which made me nervous even about the prospect of standing still.

We took the train to Kawasaki, an industrial slum inhabited by poor Koreans. The streets were shabby and smelled of fermented cabbage and open sewers. But the laws were looser than in Tokyo, hence the many strip clubs and sex shows. Our destination was called Yamashita Paradise, misspelled as "Paradize" in flashing neon lights. A young man with frizzy permed hair and tattooed eyebrows, a not uncommon look among low-ranking

Anzu in the dressing room of the striptease theater

yakuza, ushered us inside. Since this was not a kinpun show, there was no need to be covered in gold paint. For my number with Anzu, the female half of Dance Love Machine, all I needed to wear was a tiny scarlet jockstrap. Anzu, in a minuscule bikini bottom of sparkling silver, told me not to worry about a thing. She was a skilled modern ballet dancer as well as a Butoh performer. She would do all the work. All I needed to do was to catch her in my arms at the end of the dance.

The stage felt clammy. There was a smell of stale beer and cigarettes. I could hear the men in the audience chatting loudly but could not see them because of the colored spotlights shining in our faces. Tom Jones began to sing "It's Not Unusual," I struck up a manly pose, a bit like Charles Atlas in the body-building ads, and Anzu started her sinuous dance around me. Everything seemed to be going fine; I felt almost relaxed. I could get used to this kind of thing. Alas, relief can turn to complacency in seconds. My attention flagged just at the wrong moment. Anzu flung herself into my waiting arms, Tom Jones sang his last notes ("It's not unusual to find out that I'm in love with you, whoa-oh-oh-oh"); I was taken by surprise and made the only mistake I could possibly have made: I dropped her onto the stage floor.

There was no booing from the audience—just a stunned silence, which was worse. It was as if my embarrassment filled the dark void, like a ghastly miasma. Nothing was said in the dressing room, as we hastily put on our clothes for the trip back to Tokyo. Once again I apologized to Anzu in the train. She smiled thinly. I never performed in a cabaret again.

HAVING SPENT MORE THAN two years at least nominally as a film
school student, and spurred by Maro and others that I should do
something, make something of my own, I decided it was time
to try my hand at making a short movie. The resulting script of
First Love, or *Hatsukoi* in Japanese, showed all the marks of a
young man who had seen too many *roman porno* films. Even
the irony of the title itself was heavy as a sledgehammer.

My friend Tsuda played the leading character, a solitary
figure in the big city craving a woman's love. One day, walking
the streets, he is approached by a young woman who promises
to show him a good time. They go to his tiny apartment, shot
on location in my living/bedroom in Mejiro. He believes that
he has found a girlfriend at last. She asks him for money when
the good time is over. In a blind rage, he kills her.

Kin-san, my friend from the Nichidai film school, shot the
movie on 16mm film. An apprentice dancer from the Asbestos
Studio, called Miho, whom I was madly in love with, played the
girl. Small and lithe, Miho was studying French literature and
performing most nights at a large burlesque theater near the
Ginza, where Ri Koran, the Manchurian movie star, gave con-
certs during the war, before turning into Shirley Yamaguchi
after Japan's surrender.

I cannot blame Tsuda, Miho, or Kin-san for the failure of
this morbid study of alienation. The story was full of unearned
darkness. I cannot even claim that it was a true expression
of my own deepest feelings. The film might have been more

interesting if that had been true. It was just a pale reflection of the *ero, guro, nansensu* that I had been lapping up in Tokyo. Others had expressed the same sort of thing with more wit. *Hatsukoi* should never have been shown to anyone.

And yet it was. Perhaps gaijin's privilege kicked in once more. Kawakita Kazuko, the daughter of Kawakita Nagamasa, the film producer in wartime Shanghai, ran a film distribution company called Furansu Eigasha. She had handled films by Visconti, Fellini, Wim Wenders, and Godard. Outside Japan she had introduced audiences to Oshima's work. Kazuko was one of the most attractive and important figures in the movie business. She was also unfailingly generous. And so she offered to screen my movie at her company, in the same room where films by Oshima, Chris Marker, and Godard were shown.

Kazuko, Donald Richie, and I settled into our seats for the screening. When the lights went up after fifteen minutes, there was a short silence. "Well," Kazuko said brightly, "I think it's time to go for dinner."

NOT SO LONG AFTER THAT, Maro decided that I should be in the next Dairakudakan show. But perhaps with my cabaret performance in mind, he would mercifully spare me the embarrassment of acting as a dancer. We would embark on a short tour through Japan, first to Nagoya, then to Kyoto. My simple role, Maro reassured me, was to stick my head through a window onstage and imitate Adolf Hitler. The title of the piece was *Arashi,* meaning "Tempest." The show lasted about as long as Ravel's *Bolero,* which was played at high volume throughout, as Maro's star dancers, including Amagatsu, Anzu, Murobushi Ko, and "Carlotta" Ikeda, squirmed and cowered and silently screamed in the requisite Butoh manner, their bodies coated with rice flour and streaks of bloodred paint.

There was little point in rehearsing an improvisation of the Führer's tirade, and so I, too, did the same physical exercises as the dancers. This made me feel fitter without necessarily improving my proficiency. Ravel's *Bolero* is not an easy piece to sit through once without getting restless. Hearing it over and over can become a torment. But the spectacle of cadaverous bodies straining to come to life in different variations, and Maro's solo dance as a swaying mummy with black eyes in a chalky face like some creature of the night, was, to say the least, arresting.

We traveled to Nagoya in a large van. Everyone was in good cheer. Amagatsu cracked jokes. Maro's mournful features creased with laughter as memories of former tours were recalled. It was one of those brisk sunny Japanese fall days, when everything looks sharply etched like a woodblock print. Even Mount Fuji, which is usually hidden in clouds, stood out like an ice-cream cone against the almost cobalt-blue sky. One of the male dancers rather ostentatiously turned his back to the window, exclaiming to no one in particular that there was nothing pretty about Mount Fuji.

Fuji, as much of an icon of Japan as the Eiffel Tower is of Paris, has a peculiar status, with right-wing connotations. In the world of Shinto, many rocks, rivers, and other forces of nature are considered to be divine, but Mount Fuji is the most sacred of all. When Shinto, which began as a form of nature worship—with rituals to ensure fertility and good harvests, and so on—became a state cult in the late nineteenth century, it came to be associated with militarism, ultranationalism, and worship of the emperor, until this type of thing was banned under the American occupation after the war.

I don't think the dancer who turned his back on the holy mountain did so as a form of political protest against the icon's chauvinistic history. Fuji is now a harmless symbol anyway, a popular decoration on the tiled walls of public bathhouses in the days before such bathhouses began to disappear, as more and more people were able to take baths at home. More likely, his gesture was a proper Butoh-like disdain for conventional beauty. Authenticity lay in deliberate ugliness. It is true that Hijikata was inspired by his childhood in the rural northeast, but the dance pieces he created didn't celebrate the splendors of nature. They were more redolent of backbreaking work in the rice fields and bodies shrinking from the icy winds of endless winters.

Nagoya is the neatest city in Japan, and perhaps the most boring. Like almost every other place, it was pretty much destroyed in the last years of the war. But unlike Tokyo or Osaka, whose rebirths were as capricious as human life, Nagoya was the only city to be rebuilt according to a carefully worked-out plan. It is a city of straight and wide avenues, as rational as a mathematical equation. Nagoya's main distinction is the invention of the pachinko pinball machine, which was ubiquitous all over Japan. There were many more pachinko parlors than cinemas, let alone bookstores. In the 1970s you could hear them from a long way off, the noise of cascading silver balls combining with the deafening background military music—the Imperial Navy's "Warship March" being especially popular.

But not everything in Nagoya was soulless and new. We were to perform at a tumbledown old theater, mostly used by traveling groups like the one I had photographed near the old execution grounds in Tokyo. It has probably been pulled down by now. The wooden building had a musty odor of tatami mats that hadn't been replaced often enough. The stage was on the ground floor. We all slept on the ratty tatamis in a large room above the theater. At night that is also where we ate, sang songs, and drank too much.

Since the local press or radio stations wouldn't take any notice of a Butoh troupe arriving in town, we had to do our own publicity, which meant driving our van through the main streets, advertising our performance through a megaphone. I had often been annoyed, as were most Japanese even if they rarely showed it, by the ubiquitous sound trucks in Tokyo of uniformed right-wing fringe groups, mostly small-time gangsters, bellowing militaristic slogans and playing wartime martial songs. But I enjoyed addressing crowds in this manner. It felt good to hear my own amplified voice booming at the modern buildings.

We parked the van near the front entrance of Nagoya's main railway station, where Amagatsu, Carlotta, and the others startled commuters by doing a half-naked Butoh dance, while I used the megaphone to invite people to come see us perform at 7:30.

By 7:15 the theater was so full that it felt dangerous to me. This was not an unusual situation. I had been to performances inside small wooden buildings, packed with people, with kerosene stoves to keep us warm and no fire escapes. For a highly organized society, with rules for everything and an almost universal fear of the unexpected, there was a curious recklessness about the way some things were done. It was as though without clear rules, people felt no need to use common sense. I was surprised at first to see how nobody would jaywalk, even without a single car in sight, but would think nothing of walking straight through heavy traffic in the absence of a red light.

Our performance in Nagoya was a success. Death and rebirth were painfully reenacted to the sounds of *Bolero*. Even though only my face was seen, peering through a window, around about the time when the trumpets come on, I was still fully made up in white and wore nothing but a jockstrap. Pulling Hitler-like grimaces, I did my rant in cod German, as Maro swayed back and forth in a tattered red kimono, and the entire group danced for the finale, with lots of dried brown fish attached to red cords, like arteries or intestines, dropping to the stage.

The party afterward was held upstairs in our sleeping quarters, where long tables were laid out, covered with plates of delicious raw fish provided by a local Butoh fan who happened to be a fishmonger. All that remains in my memory is a blur of florid faces, singing and drinking, and laughing. One of the dancers climbed on the table and did a slow grind, while three of the women dancers improvised a kind of French cancan to the sound of our rhythmic clapping. A friendly jazz drummer tapped along furiously with chopsticks on his beer glass. Nobody got hurt. We rolled out our bedding at around three in the morning.

The venue in Kyoto, called the Seibu Kodo, was even more remarkable than the old theater in Nagoya. It was a huge barn of a place with a traditional Japanese-style roof, on which there were still traces of the three painted stars of Orion's belt. Frank Zappa had performed in this hall the year before and declared that it was the craziest place he had ever played in. That must have been an exaggeration. But the Seibu Kodo's history was indeed curious. Built for Kyoto Imperial University in 1937, the year that Japan invaded China, to commemorate the birth of Emperor Hirohito, it was taken over in the early 1970s by student radicals and had since become a venue for rock-and-roll and theater groups.

After the rehearsal, just as the sun went down, casting a burnt-orange glow on the yellow-starred roof, naked dancers in rice flour and ash stood around the palms and cypress trees like figures in a fairy tale. I could only gaze in wonder at the beauty of the scene, made more surreal by the faint sound of *Bolero* drifting from the hall, when my girlfriend in the black leather trousers, the one who liked Roxy Music, said she was going back to our dormitory. She had come down from Tokyo especially to see us perform. Her name was Chieko. She wasn't feeling well.

The dorm was in a rather dilapidated prewar university building. When I caught up with Chieko a few hours later, she was clearly upset by something. She wouldn't tell me what it was. Only weeks later, when we met up again in Tokyo, she blurted out that in my absence, one of the dancers had tried to push her onto the tatami. When she protested, he said: "You do it with a gaijin, so why not with one of us."

The show went even better than in Nagoya. The dorm had been cleared for the party. Amagatsu was being his amiable self, moving around the room, pouring drinks and telling jokes. Maro was beaming, as though on a high. We sat in a large circle, passing around beer and whiskey and flasks of sake. A fish stew was boiling away in a braiser. Chieko appeared to have recovered. We sang old high school songs, of which I never learned all the words, like students around a campfire. There was dancing. Urged, as is customary on such occasions, to contribute to the entertainment, I sang the theme song from a well-known yakuza movie called *Theater of Life:* "Throw away our chivalrous duty, and the world will go dark . . ."

Things began to wind down around one in the morning. One or two people were already curled up in their futons. Maro was smoking and chatting with one of the female dancers, Anzu perhaps. I saw Amagatsu staring from the other side of the room at a young male dancer sitting close to where I was. Amagatsu looked pale and wasn't smiling. All of a sudden he grabbed one of the large empty sake bottles and flung it with full force at the man. The bottle crashed onto his forehead with a nasty clunk, like hitting a coconut with a hammer. Blood began to gush from his wound, splashing my shirt.

I don't mind violence in the movies but never fail to be shaken by the real thing. I wanted to leave. Whatever personal motives Amagatsu might have had, or whatever group dynamics I had missed, I didn't want to know. I stood up and stomped out into the dark night, with Chieko, loyally, in tow. My blood-soaked shirt felt cold and clammy in the autumn chill. The stars were shining brightly, as we walked through the old streets of

Kyoto, wooden houses on both sides, in search of a place to stay. As my shock wore off, I rather relished the romance of the situation.

I don't know what the keeper of the shabby little inn, whom we roused from her bed by knocking loudly on the sliding bamboo door, must have thought when she saw the foreigner in his bloody shirt with a young Japanese woman. But by some miracle she let us stay the night.

Chieko went back to Tokyo the next morning. I returned to the dorm, feeling a little sheepish about my self-righteous exit. Maro, who had clearly witnessed such scenes many times before, was keen to soothe ruffled feathers. He said "I'm sorry" to me in English. There seemed to be no more ill feeling between Amagatsu and the young dancer, whose head was swaddled in bandages, like a turban. I explained how I felt about physical violence, how much I disliked it, and so on. Maro nodded, and said that violence was not good. But my physical squeamishness must have seemed at odds with the intense physicality of Butoh. One of the dancers made this clear when he turned to me and said, in a mixture of surprise and some disdain: "So, Buruma, you still believe in words."

SEVEN

Like many great cities, Tokyo is really a collection of villages. Each district, every neighborhood, has its own atmosphere: the Ginza with its plush department stores and expensive boutiques; Ikebukuro, a little louche, with petty gangsters and transvestite prostitutes lurking in the backstreets behind the railway station; Harajuku, modish and full of teenagers; Kanda, literary, with the smells of old-fashioned Chinese restaurants and used books.

By the 1970s, the artistic and cultural center of gravity had moved almost entirely to the west, away from the old popular areas in the eastern "low city," the *shitamachi,* along the Sumida River. Parts of the low city still had some seedy charm, but the old striptease joints and burlesque houses near the temple to the goddess of mercy in Asakusa had become sordid relics, attracting a sparse audience of old men and bums looking for a place to nap. The Asakusa Opera, a beacon of modernism before the war, was long gone. Once-famous movie houses, like the Meigaza, had become shabby venues for porno films and endlessly rerun gangster pictures. There was still a tiny Korean area in Asakusa, where you could buy fermented vegetables pickled with red peppers kept in plump brown earthenware pots. Korean immigrants had been lynched there in 1923 by Japanese mobs in a murderous rage after the terrible earthquake of that year (Koreans, idiotically, were accused of poisoning the water supplies). The Arizona, a Western-style restaurant where the great literary flaneur Nagai Kafu would have his pork cutlet for lunch every day until he died in 1959, was still in business. And so was the line of stalls selling Buddhist trinkets, cheap kimonos, and sweet dumplings that led to the temple. But the erstwhile glamour of the *shitamachi,* celebrated by Kafu, only lived on as myth.

The action had long since shifted to Shinjuku, especially the dense areas around the east exit of the main railway station. Shinjuku had a mythology of its own, as the capital of the counterculture in the 1960s. Hipsters, like the young Maro Akaji, hung out at the Fugetsudo coffee bar (gone by the time I arrived in Japan). Student protesters fought the riot police in the wide avenues running between the station and the former red-light areas of Kabukicho.

Kara Juro and his Situation Theater set up their red tent in front of Hanazono Shrine, next to a warren of alleys called the Golden Gai that had once been filled with brothels and had since turned into tiny bars plastered with movie and theater posters. With no room for more than ten people at the most, these places were frequented by artists, writers, journalists, filmmakers, and an assortment of nocturnal hangers-on, arguing about art and revolution, and scrapping in drunken feuds that only the true cognoscenti could possibly understand. Oshima Nagisa celebrated all this in a vivid but dated movie entitled *Diary of a Shinjuku Thief* (1969), a sly homage to Jean Genet featuring, among other Shinjuku legends, Kara Juro and his actors standing on their heads in front of Shinjuku station, dressed in loincloths, displaying fake gangster tattoos, and describing themselves to the camera as theatrical vagabonds.

The embers of that age still glowed a little in the 1970s. Memories were fresh. There were enough people around who had been there when the students ran amok or when Kara's actors staged a violent attack in the summer of 1969 on Terayama's Tenjo Sajiki headquarters, after Terayama, by way of a black joke, had sent Kara a funeral wreath on the opening night of his new play. During my time in Japan, there were still occasional brawls, but there was no more talk of revolution. Now, as I am writing this in 2016, the Golden Gai bars have been abandoned by their old clientele and become a destination, well advertised in Lonely Planet guides, for young Western tourists.

I continued to meet Terayama from time to time at the first Tenjo Sajiki studio in the middle of Shibuya—the one that was assaulted by Kara's people in 1969. This was perhaps the flashiest entertainment district of Tokyo, a cacophonous hub of department stores, bars, restaurants, short-time hotels, and movie theaters, a kind of neon-lit souk of commercial pleasure, like Shinjuku, but without any of its revolutionary aura. Shibuya was never a center of counterculture, but to a small-town boy like Terayama, longing for metropolitan escape, it must have looked like an urban nirvana.

That first Tenjo Sajiki office and studio still bore the marks of 1960s hippy-dippy fashion. The facade of the building had a huge clown's face stuck onto it, as well as plastic limbs, various painted mannequins, and signs of the zodiac. Inside were a coffee bar, a small theater, and a tiny office, where Terayama would receive people. He was always courteous, even friendly, but in a watchful way. Like Andy Warhol, he liked to gather misfits and exhibitionists around him and use them as props for a world of his own creation. He had the erotic imagination of an obsessive voyeur. But as a man he exuded coolness, professional efficiency, and distance. He was a loner in his theatrical lair. Our conversations were usually brief. He would sit back in his leather chair and make gnomic statements, like: "The Japanese are all masochists at heart."

In the late 1970s, when Shibuya began to shed its rougher edges and became the mecca of teenage culture, Terayama moved his company to Azabu, a quieter, more expensive area. Gone were the zodiac signs and plastic dolls. The new office-studio was slick with chrome furniture and chic black walls. It suited him. Like so much else that began in the 1960s, the Tenjo Sajiki had grown up and become more polished, more urbane. Terayama always retained his distinct northeastern accent, but it was as though years of living his metropolitan dream had gradually washed away the earthiness of his origins. (The old Tenjo Sajiki studio in Shibuya is now a fancy office building of steel and glass.)

Kara Juro and his entourage could not have been more different. I can't recall exactly when I first met Kara. In any case,

I had seen several of his plays performed in various parts of Tokyo in that crimson tent. I was still involved with Maro Akaji's Dairakudakan. Kara rarely took kindly to his star actors leaving the fold, which he saw as a form of betrayal, but there seemed to have been no animosity between Maro and Kara. Nor did they have much occasion to meet, or bother to see each other's productions. They lived in separate worlds now. This was common among Japanese theater groups. They operated a bit like gangs, or clans, which sometimes clashed but usually stuck to their own turf, feigning supreme indifference to what anyone else was up to.

My entry into Kara's world was on a Sunday afternoon. That I do remember. I had called him one day, prompted perhaps by Ritsaert ten Cate, who presumably wanted me to contact Kara to look into the possibility of a trip to the Mickery Theater. Kara immediately invited me over to his house, which he shared with his wife, Ri Reisen, and their young son, Gitan. Ri was a tough Korean-Japanese beauty with a gravelly voice and the pout of a tropical fish. She played all the leading female roles in Kara's plays. They had performed together since they first met as students. Kara's productions had few other parts for women. I was told that Ri did not welcome the presence of potential rivals. It was also whispered that she had ample reason for caution. Their comfortable detached house, in a quiet western suburb far from the hubbub of Shinjuku or Shibuya, had a studio on the second floor.

On one side of the studio, sitting on flat cushions, were Kara, Ri, and some of the senior actors. I recognized Kobayashi

Rehearsing a play at the Situation Theater studio

Kaoru, tall and sad-eyed, with short-cropped frizzy hair. Kobayashi, who was exactly my age, usually played the kinds of parts that Maro had performed in the 1960s: odd-looking sinister obsessives of one kind or another. Friends called him by his first name, Kaoru. Nezu Jinpachi, on the other hand, lithe and darker-skinned, a little myopic but more conventionally handsome, was always called by his surname. Nezu, whom Kara once described as the Tokyo James Dean, was invariably cast as the romantic lead, embarking on tangled quests for ghost-like women, or long-lost siblings, all played by Ri, who was about five years older. Kara himself played haunted eccentrics who usually fell victim to the machinations of more aggressive characters.

Kara silently beckoned me to grab a cushion and sit down next to him. The room smelled of wood and sweat. A number of actors were rehearsing a scene from one of his shorter plays. Some of the men were dressed in tattered uniforms of the Imperial Japanese Army. A young woman in white underwear— not Ri, obviously—was screaming her head off. For the rest, my memories are unreliable; I might have confused some of the imagery with other Kara plays. But I think a fight broke out between the men. I know there was a huge amount of shouting, and faces were contorted with rage, or wide-eyed with fear or wonder. Puns and other wordplays came tumbling out at enormous speed. Bloodred water from a milk bottle was tipped over the head of one of the men. A blind figure in a white coat and dark glasses tapped his cane and sang a song from a popular movie to the greasy sound of saxophones from a tape recorder. All of a sudden the fighting soldiers were transformed into a backing chorus, waving their arms and shaking their legs like show dancers.

I had trouble following the words, let alone the plot. To call this spectacle overacted would be a total understatement. The mayhem on the improvised stage of beer crates and frayed curtains was like that of a lunatic asylum. But what looked like anarchy was in fact a meticulously planned act of stylization. The actors used their bodies like dancers. Every emotion was expressed in an exaggerated physical manner. There was nothing remotely traditional about what I was seeing. But it was as though Kabuki had been reinvented in a completely modern fashion. (I wasn't around at the time, of course, but one of Kara's biggest stars in the 1960s was a handsome figure named

Yotsuya Simon, who specialized in glamorous female roles. Simon later became even more famous as a maker of spooky dolls of dreamy nude adolescents.)

Despite all the commotion onstage, I couldn't keep my eyes off Kara himself. Totally absorbed in the action, his mouth soundlessly repeated every word, with an occasional smile at the wittiness of his own lines, while his small dark eyes burned with a weird intensity. There was nothing cool or detached about Kara. One sensed a volcanic energy in the man that was attractive and a little alarming. He was short and thickset, like a sturdy peasant, with the soft baby-face of a Japanese Orson Welles, a face that contained the sweetness as well as the cruelty of an overimaginative child.

So, he said, after the rehearsal was over, what did you think? We had gone downstairs. It was a chilly afternoon, so we placed our feet under an electric blanket covering the low table on the tatami floor. The room was filled with members of the group. Kara motioned with his chin for one of the younger actors to open a bottle of whiskey. The hierarchy was clear, even to me as a newcomer. When Kara spoke, everyone listened. Sometimes Kaoru, or Nezu, or another senior member of the group, would recollect some story from past performances. The younger actors just smiled and nodded their approval. Their main role was to make sure our glasses were filled at regular intervals, or be the butt of affectionate jokes. I felt as though I was in the midst of a close-knit family, with a patriarch, and in this case a matriarch, too—Ri had no trouble speaking up. None of the actors lived in the house, so far as I could tell, but there was an atmosphere of communal living.

The Japanese have an expression for human relations that are sticky with the mutual obligations and dependencies of the collective life. They use the English word "wet." Traditional Japanese family relations are "wet." Yakuza gangs are "wet." Behavior that is more detached, more individualistic, often associated with a Western way of life, is "dry." Terayama Shuji was "dry." Kara was most definitely "wet."

Wetness in Kara's style was not just metaphorical. Not only did Kara often use water in his stage business—floods cascading from the rafters, or actors emerging from tubs of water, or sometimes from an actual river or canal—but images of oceans, pools, or swamps often recurred in his writing. Actors in the Situation Theater were extremely physical with one another. They screamed, they fought, they cried. This was very different from the Tenjo Sajiki, despite their street theater that sometimes provoked violent confrontations. Terayama used the individual eccentricity of his players, but mostly as human pieces in the chess game of his imagination. Visually, they were always interesting, but they didn't act together so much as pose or speak in monologues, like figures absorbed in their own dreams.

As a habitual outsider who could never fully commit to any kind of family, group, or circle, I should have been much more comfortable with Terayama's world than with Kara's. And yet I was instantly attracted to Kara and his group. The coolness of the Tenjo Sajiki and the kinky eroticism of Terayama's fantasy world had inspired me to come to Tokyo. But after almost three years in Japan this was no longer as satisfying as before. I now yearned for the heat of Kara's wetter universe.

I must have mentioned Ten Cate's hope to bring the Situation

Theater to Amsterdam. Kara thanked me for relaying the invitation but did not express any interest. Why should they go west? He told me extraordinary stories about tours in recent years to Seoul, Bangladesh, and Palestinian refugee camps in Syria and Lebanon. The actors had learned to speak their lines in Korean, Bengali, and Arabic, crammed into their memories in a few months. I questioned, rather impudently, how much the audiences in Dhaka or Beirut had understood. "Oh, about forty percent," Kara replied, his face creased with amusement.

After the second bottle of whiskey had been emptied, Kara ordered one of the young players to bring out some snacks. Plates of pickled vegetables and dried octopus appeared from the kitchen. Nezu recalled an incident in one of the Palestinian camps. They had performed a much-revised version of *Kaze no Matasaburo,* the first play I had seen in Japan a few years earlier. For the performance in the camps the villain in the piece was dressed up as Moshe Dayan, and the Japanese imperial intelligence agency had been transformed into the Mossad. Palestinian commandos were invited to appear as extras onstage. Children threw stones at the actor dressed up as General Dayan. Kara's eyes widened at the memory of this remarkable occasion. Like us, the Palestinians are a people of vagabonds, he said. He looked at me in wonder and said in a low voice: "And some of the men started to shoot off their Kalashnikovs. We were worried there would be a riot!" Everyone howled with laughter.

I wondered what had drawn Kara to the Middle East. The reason for performing in Seoul was not hard to understand. Partly through his wife, he felt a kinship with Koreans. Often, during late-night drinking sessions at home, Kara would play sentimental Korean ballads on his tape recorder and wipe tears from his eyes with the back of his hand. The Palestinian cause in Japan might have had something to do with the residue of pan-Asian sentiment, once the staple of wartime propaganda, that ran through the Japanese Left of the 1960s and '70s, a romantic attachment to struggles of non-Western peoples against "U.S. imperialism." Kara had friends connected to the Japanese Red Army. One of them, a filmmaker named Adachi Masao, was living in exile in Beirut. Kara had acted in some of his movies, which were an odd but not untypical mixture of revolutionary attitudes and violent pornography. In one of the most memorable films, written by Adachi and directed by another radical director, named Wakamatsu Koji, Kara played an impotent serial killer who tortures several nurses to death in a hospital ward. Adachi had helped Kara with introductions to the Palestinians.

Kara's views on the Palestinian conflict seemed to be entirely based on emotion, the type of feeling that made him cry when he listened to Korean ballads. Whatever his plays were about, they could not be reduced to agitprop. Ending a play with a cry to "kill the Zionists!," as Kara did in Syria and Lebanon, would have been unthinkable in Japan. Political agitation was not his thing. Kara liked to provoke through black humor and turning logic on its head. But I think he saw theatrical possibilities in real-life popular revolts. Whipping Palestinians into a frenzy by impersonating Moshe Dayan was just the kind of effect that he relished. "The situation," he would often cry, "it is all about the situation." Kara's student thesis had been about Jean-Paul Sartre, a hero of the anti-imperialist Japanese Left. What he meant, I think, is that he wanted sparks to fly by matching his provocative theater to real-life drama. If the public confused them, so much the better.

I must confess that I had not thought any of this through during that first wintry evening at Kara's house. I was amused when Kara talked about shooting a Kalashnikov himself in one of the Palestinian camps. It was fun when everyone sang songs from Kara's plays, clapping in rhythm, like Spaniards do with flamenco songs. Woozy with Suntory whiskey I clapped along with the others, as Kara sang the "Ali Baba" song from his 1967 play of that title. I remembered it from Oshima's movie, *Diary of a Shinjuku Thief.* Kara was impressed that I, a gaijin after all, knew his song. The actors joked that I had to be a "spy." I was happy to participate in this warm wet world. It felt less like spying than like the beginning of another immersion.

MADE TO FEEL welcome by Kara and his players, I began to hang out with them regularly. We would get drunk at Kara's house on the first day of the New Year. I attended rehearsals in the studio. And I joined the small entourage that accompanied Kara on visits to his favorite bar in Shinjuku's Golden Gai. Ri was never a part of these excursions. This was an all-male thing. Kara was the *oyabun,* literally father figure, a word commonly used for gang bosses. We were his *kobun,* his children, or gang members. There was a swagger about Kara as he entered his favorite haunts, and following him afforded a strange pleasure, a sense of belonging, even of reflected power.

We always frequented the same tiny bar, called Maeda, which catered mostly to theater people. Film people went to another place, called La jetée, after the French cult movie directed by Chris Marker, who had had an affair with the woman who owned the bar. Writers and journalists went to yet another place. Strangers rarely strolled into these Golden Gai bars uninvited. Turf was carefully guarded here. The preferred drink was whiskey and water, *mizuwari*, kept in personal bottles that were marked with the names of regular patrons.

Maeda had been the scene of some of Kara's famous brawls. On one often-recounted occasion he had beaten up the novelist Nosaka Akiyuki, who had just won an important literary prize. After too many *mizuwaris*, Nosaka, usually a gentle figure, taunted Kara that he had never won the prize. This stirred up the gang boss in Kara, like the time he received Terayama's funeral wreath. I had seen it happen on other occasions. His baby-face would go livid and punches would fly.

My own role in Kara's entourage was unclear. I was obviously not one of the actors, nor had I accomplished anything important as an artist or intellectual. At that time I was supplementing my scholarship money with stints as a film reviewer for the *Japan Times*, a freelance translator, and an occasional assistant to Magnum photographers who came to Japan to shoot corporate annual reports. My main asset in Kara's eyes was that I was a rare gaijin interested in Japanese movies and contemporary theater, and above all in Kara himself. A frequent topic of conversation was the question of talent, who had it and who didn't. This was very important to him. To be a person without talent was to be beyond the pale. You could be a rogue, but you had to have talent. Kara might have spotted some possibilities in me, but if I had any talent at all, it was as yet unclear for what. The fact that John Schlesinger was my uncle was perhaps an asset of a kind. Kara much admired *Midnight Cowboy*.

One night at Maeda I spotted the composer Takemitsu Toru sitting in the corner of the bar, nursing his glass of *mizuwari*, with a faulty neon light flickering on his bird-like features through a small window. Although he was among the greatest composers of his time, Takemitsu was quite shy. But he loved to sing Frank Sinatra songs after a few drinks. Not many words were exchanged between Kara and Takemitsu. Then Kara said something about his talent for singing, and Takemitsu's sweet baritone voice, surprisingly voluminous for such a small man, filled the bar with "Fly Me to the Moon."

Japanese artists of Kara's generation had a complicated attitude toward Western, and especially American, culture. Resentment, envy, and admiration were there in equal measure. I am convinced that Kara's pan-Asian sentiments had something to do with his "gaijin complex." Like Takemitsu, or Oshima, or indeed Terayama, he had experienced the national humiliation of being occupied by white men who were richer, physically larger on the whole, and more powerful than they were. Japanese men were particularly sensitive about this. Their sense of masculinity had been offended.

It was in fact Nosaka Akiyuki, the novelist Kara had beaten up at Maeda, who expressed this most acutely in an extraordinary short story called "American Hijiki." The main character is a young man called Toshio who grew up during the war being told by his teachers that Westerners were physically and mentally inferior to the tougher Japanese race. He was shocked to find out that this was not necessarily so. Years after the occupation was officially over, with a mixture of awe and bitterness, Toshio remembered a GI with "arms like logs" and his "manly buttocks encased in shiny uniform pants . . . Ah, no wonder Japan lost the war."

One day Toshio is obliged to entertain a middle-aged American businessman on a visit to Tokyo. The visitor, named Higgins, fondly recalls his time as a soldier during the occupation. They attend a live sex show, where Japan's "Number One" will show off his prowess. Alas, Japan's "Number One" has an off night and isn't up to the task. All the humiliation suffered during those early postwar years comes flooding back, as Toshio and his smug white guest witness the collapse of Japanese manhood.

That same night, when Takemitsu sang "Fly Me to the Moon," while we were facing our *mizuwaris* on the bar, Kara asked me which Western playwrights I liked. This, too, was a regular feature in our conversations, the relative merits of this artist or that. It was a way of bonding over shared enthusiasms. Gaijin complex or not, Kara's taste was never narrowly provincial. I mentioned a few names. Then he said, somewhat to my surprise: "You know who I like? Tennessee Williams. He's really good, isn't he?" The other actors sitting at the bar nodded silently.

I could not quite square Tennessee Williams's tender

Southern Gothic sensibility with Kara's raucous surrealism. *The Glass Menagerie* seemed a long way from *Kaze no Matasaburo*. I tried to see why timid Laura's private dream world of glass objects would appeal to the author of roughhousing neo-Kabuki. It did not come to me till later that there was indeed a connection. For Kara, too, had a private dream world, filled with cruelty and tenderness, which was the basis of almost all his plays. As with Williams, and indeed with Terayama, this basis was formed by memories of his early childhood.

Kara was born in the heart of Tokyo's *shitamachi*. Before the war his family had moved into a wooden row house in Shitaya Mannencho, a neighborhood between Ueno and Asakusa, not far from the red-light district of Yoshiwara and the Sanya skid row. Mannencho used to be one of the most notorious slums in Tokyo, already known in the Edo Period as a nest of ragpickers, pimps, ditchdiggers, petty gamblers, and fairground entertainers. Kara's family was actually more middle class, but his grandfather had dissipated the family fortune, which is why they had moved to this squalid area. To escape from the wartime bombing, Kara was evacuated to the countryside for a year. When he returned in 1945, at the age of five, most of the *shitamachi* had been obliterated, although oddly enough his own family house had been spared. Kara would often recall the pleasure of playing in the rubble with a clear view all the way to Mount Fuji. He also loved to tell stories about the transvestite hookers who lived in public toilets and fought one another in turf battles with knives. Or the *pan pan* girls, whores who specialized in luring American soldiers for quick sex in the ruins. He remembered the petty gangsters who prowled the streets, and the tofu seller's daughter who hanged herself after gnawing the bones of her stillborn baby. He recalled the impoverished army veterans eking out a living by selling hot snacks in the street. His mother would take him to the jerry-built theaters in Asakusa, where he saw the popular comedians of the day and dreamed of being one of the Three Musketeers or the Count of Monte Cristo.

Kara was by his own account a quiet bookish boy who got excellent grades in school. But the place he grew up in would shape his macabre imagination forever. However much he mixed up Greek myths or Japanese fairy tales, or bits and pieces of French existentialism, with pop culture and contemporary events, the extraordinary characters he observed in Shitaya Mannencho after the war would always keep popping up in his plays like ghosts that refused to slip away. They were the pieces of his glass menagerie, which he arranged and rearranged with every new drama.

The world that Kara knew as a child was of course long gone when I lived in Tokyo. *Shitamachi* had been cleaned up considerably. Even the wooden houses that had miraculously survived in Mannencho looked quaintly traditional rather than poor. Kara certainly felt no nostalgia for it. I often heard him lament the fact that he had been born in Tokyo and not in the rural northeast like Terayama or Hijikata. He often felt that Tokyo culture was false and rootless. His *nostalgie de la boue* was for the muddier spheres of village Japan, still haunted by spirits, or the poorer, darker parts of Asia or the Middle East, such as Korea or Palestine, where struggles for life and death seemed more authentic, or at least more dramatic, than in prosperous, boom-time Japan.

Perhaps it was just the mythical appeal, but like some other foreigners in Japan, I was drawn to the *shitamachi,* and often imagined moving there. The people in Ueno, Asakusa, or Shitaya seemed more down to earth than the more bourgeois denizens of the upper city. I liked the traditional air of their daily lives, their attachment to rowdy Shinto festivals, their quick sense of humor, and the general "wetness" of their culture.

Kara dismissed my *shitamachi* yearnings as misguided romantic nonsense. There was nothing of any interest there anymore, he said. All of Tokyo had become middle class. And as far as traditional popular culture was concerned, from the corny patter of kimonoed stand-up comedians to the vulgarized Kabuki theaters, celebrated by certain nostalgic intellectuals, he felt complete contempt. He couldn't understand what I saw in such things. No doubt it had something to do with being a gaijin.

He was probably right about that. But I did in fact end up being pulled into a strange dark corner of *shitamachi* culture. This came about because of my other life as a photographer.

DONALD RICHIE CALLED ME ONE DAY, not long after I met Kara. He had a proposal. Donald had long been interested in traditional Japanese tattoos, the kind that covered much of the body, from the shoulders to the knees, and sometimes to the ankles (although that was considered vulgar by the true connoisseurs). These body tattoos of mythical heroes, cherry blossoms, maple leaves, waterfalls, and fearsome protective deities had reached an extraordinary degree of refinement in Japan, while retaining a scandalous reputation among "respectable" people. Tattooed men or women were not allowed to enter most public baths, or pools. Tattoos, called *irezumi* by the uninitiated, and *horimono* by the insiders, were commonly associated with gangsters.

It is true that most yakuza sported full-body tattoos. It is also true that the earliest tattoos were brands of punishment. In some regions, several hundred years ago, a criminal would bear the ideograph for "dog" on his forehead. Outcasts, who did ritually unclean work to do with death, were often branded as well. But by the late eighteenth century these marks of shame had been transformed into a high art. Some of the greatest woodblock artists, including Hokusai and Utamaro, made designs for body tattoos in various shades of blue, red, and green.

Aside from gangsters, tattoos became popular among tough guys who prized the manliness of their occupations: firefighters, construction workers, palanquin bearers, and so on. The most popular motifs were borrowed from the fourteenth-century Chinese novel *The Water Margin,* about a gang of legendary bandit heroes, which became hugely popular in eighteenth-century Japan. Japanese toughs liked to have tattoos on their backs of Shi Jin, pronounced "Shishin" in Japanese, the brigand also known as "Nine Dragon" Shishin, because of his own elaborate tattoo of nine dragons depicted on his back.

Donald's proposal was to do a coffee-table book on traditional tattoos. The tattooist he had in mind was named Horibun II, son of the eminent tattooist Horibun I. Donald had approached him earlier, but somehow they had not hit it off. I

Horibun II with a tattoo of Nine Dragon
Shishin on his back

never discovered the reason why. Would I try to get in touch? My Japanese would surely help. If I showed proper respect, Horibun II might agree to be photographed this time. I was of course intrigued by the idea. One thing that made Horibun special is that he still practiced his craft by hand, and not with electric needles. The technique was the same as it had been in the eighteenth century. He lived and worked in a *shitamachi* area called Okachimachi, not far from where Kara grew up.

I went to see Horibun II bearing an appropriate gift of expensive rice crackers. His house was in a narrow street of small wooden houses. Firebombs must have flattened the area in 1945, but the layout of the streets was much the same as it had been for centuries. There was a tofu shop on the corner. Farther along the street men in white bandannas were busy making tatamis. Laundry was flapping in the wind on the rooftops of the two-story houses. A weepy Japanese ballad came drifting from a radio somewhere. Women gossiped in Tokyo accents. An old man in wooden sandals was tending to his bonsai. This was about as *shitamachi* as it gets.

Horibun said little at our first meeting, but was genial in a gruff kind of way. We sipped green tea in the room downstairs. A large man with rolls of fat on his neck, he wore a thick woolen waistband over a thin white shirt. I could see a bruise-like shade of blue just above the collar and flowers growing up his left arm. He told me to come back the following week. He would be working on a roof builder from Atami, a seaside resort south of Tokyo.

The second-floor studio where Horibun worked was stifling. The man from Atami was lying facedown on a blanket. He had short-cropped hair and was wearing a white loincloth. The tattooist was sitting on top of him, as though he had wrestled him to the ground. He held an ink brush in his left hand, like a cigarette between his index and middle fingers, so he could ink the tiny needles before working them into the roof builder's skin. I could see the outline, drawn with a Magic Marker, of one of the heroes from *The Water Margin*. The tight bundle of needles made a scratchy sound like the scaling of a fish as it went quickly in and out of the skin. Every so often, Horibun would wipe off the blood with a pretty colored cloth. The man said nothing much. Occasionally the pain would make him wince, but he tried not to show it. As the tattooist was working away, dipping, scratching, and wiping, he pointed out

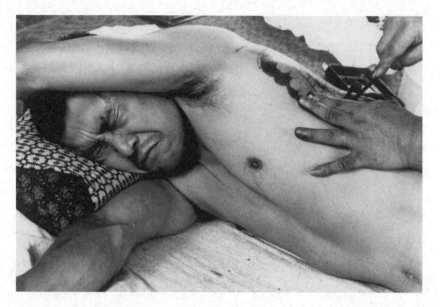

Man being tattooed

the most painful areas, where the nerves were closest to the surface, under the armpits or around the nipples. There are of course even more painful spots. I was told about a man who had the tip of his penis tattooed in the shape and color of an eggplant. But this was a specialized procedure that would only work if the pain afforded a keen pleasure. I never witnessed anything of that sort.

Horibun had taken off his white undershirt, revealing a splendid tattoo of Nine Dragon Shishin all over his back. I did not call him Horibun, or Horibun-san. In the world of traditional artisans, as hierarchical as the yakuza or indeed theatrical troupes, nomenclature was taken seriously. He was *oyakata*, chief, or patriarch, of his occupation.

I did not realize it at the time, but apparently Horibun I was still around, although gravely ill. I never saw him alive. But I attended his funeral, as a way of showing my respect. The street outside the *oyakata*'s house was lined with men in black suits. Some of them wore the crew cuts and sunglasses favored by gangsters. Large white wreaths displayed the names of donors in graceful black ideographs. Inside was an overpowering smell of incense wafting from a large number of white pots. In the middle of an elaborate Buddhist altar surrounded by white flowers was a black-and-white photograph of the stern-looking tattoo master. In front of the altar was the casket. Inside the casket was Horibun I, freshly washed the day before by his family. He wore a white kimono, and the utensils of his trade were close at hand: bottles with different shades of ink, a lacquered wooden box with an array of needles, some longer than others, neatly divided in red, blue, and green sections. Above the collar of the kimono was the waxen face of the old man; you could just see the top of his body tattoo, which was the color of faded blue jeans.

The *oyakata* was a man of few words. I never really got to know him well, but he tolerated my presence in his studio as he gradually, over many months, decorated the bodies of his clients with graceful and heroic images. I followed this process from beginning to end with the roof builder from Atami. There were others: a sushi chef, a carpenter, a construction worker, and one or two tough-looking characters introduced with a knowing chuckle to me as businessmen.

I asked them why they did it, why they wished to brand themselves for life with these indelible artworks that would bar them from social respectability? Love of tradition was the most common answer. These were conservative men. But there was something else, linked to this, something that was harder to articulate. It was most apparent when we went on excursions to famous beauty spots, where the men would pose in groups standing under freezing waterfalls, or in front of shrines, or on rocks facing the ocean. Like motorcycle clubs, the tattoos denoted a common identity, a sense of belonging. The yakuza like to present themselves as tight-knit families bound by elaborate codes of loyalty. Much of this is nonsense designed to glorify criminality. But the wetness of gang life is surely one of its attractions to men with few other ties. Even tattooed men without any yakuza connections feel a bond with people who share their taste, precisely because social opprobrium singles them out.

This familial feeling even extended to the wives. One of the men I photographed, a builder named Takeshi, told me that he had insisted that his wife get a full-body tattoo as well. According to his account, she had a green dragon curling all the way down to her thighs. But alas, he related with sadness, an unexpected cesarean section had made rather a mess of the image and now the dragon appeared to be sprouting two heads.

I liked the *oyakata* and the men he tattooed. They were warm and remarkably gentle men. But I remained firmly on the outside of their world. Horibun had kindly offered to tattoo my arm or back. Several motifs were considered: Jizo, the sacred protector of travelers, and, more oddly perhaps, dead children; or Kintaro, the boy hero, battling a giant carp; or maybe just an elegant cherry blossom design. But I foolishly turned him down. I suppose I was worried about the irreversible nature of the thing; what if I got tired of Jizo or Kintaro, or the cherry blossom?

I regret it now. And I never did move to the *shitamachi*, unlike Donald Richie, who lived in Ueno for more than three decades until the day he died in 2013, overlooking the lotus-covered pond where Kara Juro's Situation Theater performed *Kaze no Matasaburo* when I first arrived in Tokyo. Once again, I had hovered around the edges of an exclusive world, content to remain a stranger.

Takarazuka

EIGHT

cannot remember why I chose *Shojo Kamen,* or *Mask of a Virgin,* to translate. It is one of Kara's first plays and rather untypical of his work. He wrote it in 1969 for another theater group, Suzuki Tadashi's Waseda Shogekijo, who were regular visitors to the Mickery Theater.

I had never translated a play before. My writing experience was limited to movie reviews for the *Japan Times.* I still thought of myself as a photographer and aspiring filmmaker. Thinking about it now, I suppose that translating one of Kara's plays was a way to get closer to him and his imaginary world that had enchanted me. *Mask of a Virgin* was, in fact, a good choice. It is one of Kara's punchiest and most coherent plays. As in all his works, he concocted a surreal mixture of Japanese history, social satire, and a classic story reworked in his own inimitable way.

The main character is a person who actually existed, named Kasugano Yachiyo. Born in 1915, Kasugano was the main star for many years of the Takarazuka, an all-female revue company. Worshipped by countless young Japanese girls, she specialized in romantic male roles, most notably that of Heathcliff in *Wuthering Heights*. She also played Hamlet to great acclaim. Kasugano, her stage name, literally means "forever blooming spring." Short-cropped, mannish, and unmarried, Forever Blooming Spring was also known as Eternal Virgin, or so at least she is called in Kara's play. One of her last performances on the Takarazuka stage was a solo number in a dance revue entitled *Proper, Pure, Beautiful,* after the famous Takarazuka motto. Kasugano was then ninety-one. She died of pneumonia five years later. In her prime, she bore a slight resemblance to Liberace, but in a more masculine way.

Takarazuka is a teenage cult in Japan. Young girls queue all night to get tickets and scream in ecstasy or swoon when one of the stars appears. Their androgynous quality is a large part of the attraction. Dreams of romance are safe from any sexual threat. (Dark stories about lesbian domination in the troupe do circulate in Japan, but these generally don't reach the ears of the young fans.) I once took a certain camp interest in this cross-dressing phenomenon, and even went to the town of Takarazuka, where it all began in 1914. Once a mere hot spring resort near Osaka, Takarazuka is now a Lourdes for Takarazuka worshippers, who cross a pink bridge and pass a building called Illusion to get to the vast pink theater, where their dreams are acted out onstage.

During the war, the *Proper, Pure, Beautiful* revue was mobilized to make military propaganda, celebrating ideals of Asian brotherhood or the superiority of Japanese howitzers. There are photographs of the 'Zuka Girls dressed up as Imperial Navy officers dancing on a stage made up to look like the gun deck of a destroyer. Kasugano spent much of that time performing in the Japanese puppet state of Manchukuo. All this was swiftly forgotten after the war in a pink haze of Heathcliffs, Rhett Butlers, and dashing Austrian aristocrats.

In Kara's play, the Eternal Virgin has stayed behind in Manchuria after the war, living in an underground café called Nikutai, meaning Body, or Flesh. Not quite sure any longer whether she really is Heathcliff, sometimes mistaking Café Flesh for the Yorkshire Moors, Kasugano is a ghost living in the dark, searching for her body, like a theatrical vampire trying to extract life from younger flesh. The flesh is provided by Kai, a young girl in thrall to the Takarazuka cult. She acts the part of Catherine to Kasugano's Heathcliff. Their union is to be consummated in Kasugano's grave. They dance, Takarazuka style, on top of a bathtub filled with the salty tears jerked from the eyes of a thousand virgins. A businessman with memories of thirst in the firestorms that ravaged wartime Tokyo pops up begging for water. The Manchukuo chief of the secret police appears from Kasugano's murky past. In the grand finale, Kai/Catherine wears Kasugano's face as a mask. "Look!" she cries, "we've found your face!" Kasugano can't bear to look at it: "I don't want my face. I am nothing!"

There are many strands woven into this play: forgetfulness about the wartime past, the creepiness of pubescent dreams, and the confusion of identity in public performance. But above all, it is about *nikutai,* the body. Kara told me more than once that he saw acting as a form of masochism. By this he meant something quite different from Terayama's remark that Japanese were masochists. Kara was not making a sociological point about the desire to obey higher authority. Actors, in Kara's idea of theater, display their bodies to the audience. Actors were traditionally a despised section of humanity, a tradition Kara likes to invoke, but their bodies onstage gave them a special aura, what Kara calls "privilege of the flesh." Kara's mentor, Hijikata, called one of his dance performances in 1968 *Nikutai no hanran,* "revolt of the body."

This makes Kara's plays hard to translate. Even in Japanese, the text needs the physical presence of actors to make it come alive. This is true of most plays, in any language. But the difficulty of translating *Mask of a Virgin* is also a matter of cultural references. Without knowing anything about Takarazuka, or Kasugano, or Captain Amakasu, the Manchukuo secret police chief, many of the jokes lose their punch, or become altogether meaningless. Kara's zany humor also relies on clever puns, which work in Japanese, but rarely in translation.

No doubt due to my inexperience as a translator, my version of *Mask of a Virgin* failed to find a publisher.* But I was glad to have done it. Kara's theater to me was no longer just a dazzling and often bewildering spectacle. I felt that I understood him better after immersing myself in his words.

And Kara, too, seemed to be pleased, or at least intrigued. Perhaps, despite his pan-Asian sentiments, a reputation in the West still had some appeal for him. Indeed, the mixture of love

---

* A later translation, edited by Robert T. Rolf and John K. Gillespie, was published in *Alternative Japanese Drama: Ten Plays,* Honolulu: University of Hawaii Press, 1992.

and hate that marked Kara's generation, and that so often provoked their complicated feelings about Asia, made recognition
in the West all the more important.

Even though *Mask of a Virgin* languished in my desk
drawer, my status changed a little. I was no longer just a curious
gaijin, a film student, or a "spy"; I was Kara's translator. But
this new status, based on the skill to move from one language
to another, was not without a certain ambiguity. Kara, as well
as his wife, Ri, liked to point out to me that people who operated in languages other than their own were lacking in talent.
Truly talented people stuck to their own language. Proficiency
in a foreign language was a kind of performance, but without
artistic merit.

Kara couldn't stand Japanese who spoke French or English
too fluently. Such foreign-language speakers were particularly
irritating when they showed off in front of other Japanese. He
liked to imitate their way of talking in a kind of gibberish. I
could understand his aversion. I, too, found Westerners who
showed off their fluent Japanese annoying, even though, not
infrequently, that show-off would be me. This was not just a
matter of being made to feel inadequate, or, in Kara's case, a
version of the gaijin complex. It probably goes to something
deeper than that, the idea that a person speaking too fluently
in a language other than his native tongue is inauthentic, without a clear identity, an impersonator—a "spy."

There are several scenes in *Mask of a Virgin* of a ventrilo-
quist and his dummy. It is not always clear who is speaking
through whom. They swap identities. Living much of my life
among Japanese, speaking in Japanese, I sometimes felt a bit like

that dummy myself. Mimicking Japanese figures of speech, or even adopting the physical mannerisms that go with a language— the bobbing of the head in half bows when speaking on the phone, smiling all the while—sometimes made me feel like an actor in real life. One would like to think that operating in a different culture is enriching. And so it is. But there are moments when the performer in a foreign language feels that he is leaving something of himself behind, or, to put it differently, that the foreign language is just a mask, concealing something more real, whatever that something may be. I would sometimes resort to odd defense mechanisms. One method was to deliberately exaggerate the Japanese mannerisms, turning them into a kind of parody. This performance could very well come across as a form of mockery. But it had a distancing effect. It gave me the illusion, at least, that I was holding on to an essential part of myself.

I'm not sure whether Kara and Ri made their point about talent being monolingual out of tactlessness, or as a deliberate slight. The relationship between an artist and his translator is always a delicate one. An element of dependency is involved. When the translator is a foreigner in what was then still a relatively isolated culture, and thus represents a slender link to a wider world, relations can become even more complicated. It is important for the artist to make it perfectly clear that *he* is the one with the superior talent, even if the foreigner is better able to navigate between cultures.

Donald Richie had warned me about the risks of joining the entourage of famous artists. Richie's writings had done much to enhance Kurosawa's reputation in the West. As a critical pioneer, Donald had put Japanese cinema on the Western map.

Kurosawa was well aware of this and was keen to enlist Donald among his inner circle. Donald would be summoned for late-night drinking sessions, where the great man could let off steam to his intimates. But Donald chose to keep his distance, to protect his autonomy. He would observe, comment, criticize, or praise. "Wetness" was not his style.

AROUND THE TIME I translated *Mask of a Virgin,* I ceased to be a film student at Nichidai College of Art. The scholarship had come to an end. I had to make a living. Since I was a photographer, I decided I should acquire some more professional skills. The best way to do this, I thought, would be to assist an established photographer. I had already dabbled in this by assisting some Magnum photographers. But Charles Harbutt, Burt Glinn, Burk Uzzle, and others were really photojournalists, loners who didn't need much help, apart from Japanese translation. I felt I needed to learn more.

A Japanese photographer kindly introduced me to Tatsuki Yoshihiro, who needed a second assistant. Tatsuki was one of the glamour boys of the Tokyo scene, known for his fashion pictures as well as slick and stylized nudes. He had done a famous book of black-and-white photos, shot in Paris and California, of an actress named Kaga Mariko. Kaga stretched out in a French hotel room, or posing in front of Santa Monica Pier, or pulling funny faces dressed in nothing but a fur coat; these were the kinds of images that appealed to a new Japan breaking out of its isolation, eager for Western exoticism.

Tall and handsome, always sharply dressed, rather like a hip

1960s Italian movie star, Tatsuki looked the part of a fashion photographer. He drove a sleek silver and charcoal Citroën DS at a time when foreign cars were exceedingly rare. We had a quick interview in his chic studio in the middle of Roppongi, the most Westernized district of Tokyo, an area of discotheques, bars, model agencies, photo studios, and European restaurants. The first pizza place in Japan was just around the corner, initially frequented, so it was rumored, by fashion-conscious yakuza. Tatsuki glanced at my shabby flared jeans without comment and said I could start working the following week.

On the evening of that same day, we met again by chance at a swank drinks party in Roppongi, full of photographers, designers, film people, and models. Kujo Eiko, Terayama's ex-wife, whom I was still trying to teach English, had asked me to come along. This was not the kind of occasion where lowly assistants would normally mix with famous photographers, let alone chat with them informally. But Tatsuki was a man of great charm and tact. So we chatted informally over glasses of champagne. When it was time for him to leave, he whispered in my ear: "Tonight is tonight, but never forget that I'm the sensei."

It was the friendliest of warnings that this privileged gaijin should not forget his station. Sensei, in the artistic, literary, and intellectual worlds, is what an *oyakata* is among artisans, an honorific establishing superior rank.

The first assignment was a photo shoot of models dressed in expensive kimonos for a glossy ladies' magazine. My only contribution was to watch the proceedings. I can't recall the name of the first assistant. Perhaps it was Tanaka, that is,

Tanaka to the sensei, and Tanaka-san to me. We were almost exactly the same age.

Tatsuki did not have to say much to Tanaka. The odd grunt and gesture were enough. These kimono shoots were routine. Tanaka knew exactly what the sensei wanted; nothing fancy, but everything had to be just right, with spotlights picking out the intricate patterns of colorful silk kimonos being modeled by graceful matrons. The appropriate lights were quickly set up with professional calm, with silver umbrellas to reflect the flash light. I was told by Tanaka to watch carefully, so I would know what to do next time. The next time, however, was not a kimono shoot in the Roppongi studio, but a photo session in a hotel room in Yokohama, where a Eurasian starlet would be pictured in the nude, sprawled in various poses on a wide bed with gilded fittings.

The Hotel New Grand, built in the 1920s, was one of the few buildings to survive the bombings in World War II. General MacArthur once stayed there. It still had an old-world foreign ambience, brass doorknobs, high ceilings, crystal candelabras, and fake Louis XVI chairs. The alternative, in Tatsuki's oeuvre, to this kind of Western old-world atmosphere, was to pose his nudes in front of beautiful Japanese temples or traditional samurai mansions with fine tatami floors and painted lacquer screens, almost as exotic in postwar Japan as the Hotel New Grand.

Tanaka pointed to some lights with his chin and grunted with an air of great authority. Tatsuki was smoking a Gauloise cigarette on the balcony. Makeup was being applied to the starlet, who was still wrapped in a fluffy white towel. The sound of moaning foghorns in the harbor drifted in with the cool breeze from the open window. I had no idea what to do. After a painful interval, while I clumsily handled this light and that, more as a show of work than anything else, Tanaka growled, shot me a furious look, and did it himself. "Watch!" he shouted, as though to an obstinate dog who fails to accomplish a trick.

It was annoying for Tanaka to have to utter even that single word. For I was expected to learn by imitation, silently, in the way all apprentices do in Japan. You don't ask questions. Nothing is explained verbally. You acquire a skill by mimicking the movements of your teacher. It is called "learning with your body." Sushi chefs do this, too, but they have more time than I did. An apprentice chef will spend years just mixing the rice or grating ginger before he is even let near a cutting board. To repeat a menial task endlessly and suffer the abuse of your direct superior is also a form of psychological (or as some Japanese might say, spiritual) training; hardship overcome as proof of devotion.

The life of a photographer's assistant in Europe and the United States is not necessarily any easier. I was just hopelessly ill equipped for it. If I had been more practical, I would no doubt have gotten the hang of Tatsuki's lighting routines more quickly. But I wasn't. Nor was I good at anticipating orders. In short, I wasn't much good at learning with my body.

Despite having the looks of an Italian movie star, Tatsuki was in many respects an old-fashioned Japanese craftsman. His father ran a photographic portrait studio in a provincial town

on Shikoku, the smallest and least populated Japanese island. Tatsuki was one of many provincials who had come to Tokyo in the
late 1950s to make his name. Sometimes, when the day's work
was done, he would sit back on his black leather sofa, one leg
casually draped over a chrome armrest, and chat about his photography over a can of Asahi beer—or, to be more exact, we had
a beer; he preferred a Pernod with ice. "I see myself as a kind of
chef," was one of his dictums. "My task is to make the perfect
sushi roll." He used the English word "delicious," while pretending to tap a slab of tuna on a little ball of rice. It was not a bad
way to describe his photographs. The concept—all that naked
posing in piss-elegant settings—might be a trifle cheesy, but
the pictures always looked very pretty. Tatsuki was a master
technician.

My relations with Tanaka continued to be uneasy. Learning
with my body involved more than setting up studio lights.
There were various symbolic ways in which seniority would be
expressed. The way this worked is that Tatsuki would express
them to Tanaka, and Tanaka would pass them on to me. Perhaps if there had been a third assistant, I would then have had
the satisfaction of passing them on in my turn.

One of these symbolic gestures involved the unlit cigarette.
I learned about this the hard way, when Tanaka, sitting at the
wheel of Tatsuki's Citroën, waiting for the boss to emerge from
a meeting, held up a pristine Seven Stars cigarette in his left
hand. I paid no attention to this, until he suddenly barked:
"Don't you know what you're supposed to do, you idiot?" In all
innocence, I replied: "No, what?" He emitted a groan of sheer

exasperation. "When I hold up a cigarette," he finally said, with the sigh of an exhausted parent confronting a child who refuses to learn, "you light it, immediately."

I later noticed how Tanaka himself had perfected this to a fine art. He would swiftly reach for his lighter, at the very instant that Tatsuki's hand reached for his pocket to retrieve a packet of cigarettes.

Such were the trivial humiliations I should have learned to take in my stride. But there was another side to the senior-junior, *senpai-kohai,* relationship that I found even harder to put up with. Tanaka was not a man of obvious brilliance, but he meant well. Part of being a *senpai* is a duty "to take care" of the *kohai* in a more kindly way, too; firmness should be matched with shows of paternal benevolence. This usually involved drinking. Alcohol is the great lubricant of social relations in Japan. That is how people are supposed to let their guard down, speak more freely, even suspend the usual rules of hierarchy— in theory you can badmouth your boss, and all is forgiven in the light of the next day.

In practice it meant that Tanaka would take me to a bar every so often, and get drunk. The tab was always on him. Tanaka's face would get flushed, his eyes would take on the soft glow of boundless goodwill, and he would ramble on with kind, and sometimes even tearful, advice about my work, my future, the ins and outs of Japanese culture, and even my love life. I should not have been so thin-skinned. I should have protected my amour propre with a proper sense of perspective. But I found these patronizing sessions even more intolerable than being shouted at for failing to light a cigarette.

Tatsuki could not have been nicer when I told him one day that I felt I wasn't cut out to be a photographer's assistant. He understood perfectly. My ineptitude was making it hard on Tanaka too. Tatsuki wished me good luck. I still think of him fondly. We never saw each other again.

Despite my efforts as a translator, I still had not done much writing. But I was happy to review movies for the *Japan Times,* a job that Donald Richie had held for many years. I continued for about two years, until in 1979, I had grown tired of my own voice praising and dismissing the hard work of others. Most of the editors at the *Times* were Eurasians who found themselves stranded in Japan for one reason or another. The editor in chief, John Yamanaka, was half English, smoked a pipe, and spoke with a slight stammer in the fruity accent of an Edwardian gentleman. A kindly man, whose name now escapes me, edited the arts pages. He, too, was half Japanese. The other half might have been American. He got stranded at the worst possible time, at the end of 1941, when Pearl Harbor was attacked, and was drafted into the Imperial Japanese Army much against his will. He survived the terrible campaign in the jungles of Burma. With tears in his hazel eyes, he once told me how Japanese soldiers got trapped in the swamps during the monsoon, trying to escape from saltwater crocodiles by climbing up palm trees, only to fall into their hungry maws when they were too exhausted to hold on any longer.

Apart from the short film I made with my friend Tsuda, I had no experience with actual filmmaking until I was asked by a Dutch television company to make some documentaries. The VPRO was known for its adventurous programming. It had the best satirical comedies on Dutch TV. And Roelof Kiers, himself an established director of fine documentaries, started an omnibus program of short films from around the world. My contribution would be films about Japan.

I made three documentaries: one about the Japanese army, one about the life of a worker at the Yamaha motorcycle factory, and one, which I have already mentioned, about the training of an elevator girl in a department store in Osaka. My crew consisted of a cameraman and a soundman. I had help with the editing from an old hand in Japanese TV. We would spend whole nights on getting the fifteen-minute movie just right. The most successful of the three movies, or at least the one that remains most vividly in my memory, was the third one, about the elevator girl.

The department store was one of the biggest and smartest in Osaka, the kind of store where the customer would be greeted in the morning by a straight row of uniformed women standing by the door, bowing and smiling and lisping words of welcome. The elevator girls, heavily made up and lipsticked, dressed in red and cream skirt-suits, shiny white shoes, and red caps with a little black feather, were perfectly drilled. They bowed as one entered the elevator, pointed up or down with their white-gloved right hands at precisely the right angles, and announced the specialties of each floor in well-trained falsetto voices. They were human dolls, as artificial as the puppets in the Bunraku theater for which Osaka is famous. There was not one gesture or sound in their elevator performance that had not been honed to the highest perfection. I wanted to get on film exactly how this was done.

I could have chosen any of Japan's large department stores. All of them had elevator girls, dressed in the distinct uniforms of their company. The reason I picked the one in Osaka is that I had seen a photograph of a bowing machine. Someone at this store had invented a contraption that could train a woman to make a bow at precisely forty-five degrees. The machine looked a bit like a large scale, but it had a breastplate. As the person pressed against the steel plate, a moving arrow marked the degree of the bow. It could also be set for fifteen degrees, an appropriate angle for a more casual encounter, or thirty degrees, the proper angle applied to customers leaving the store.

We got to film the use of the machine, as well as the training sessions, where the falsetto voices announcing the fourth floor for women's wear and children's toys, or the tenth for pottery, household items, and art galleries, were practiced. Since the movie was shot over a period of several months, we could follow the training of one girl, named Yamada Hiroko, from start to finish. She would go through a remarkable transformation, not just from the start of her training to the moment she picked up her elevator girl license at the public ceremony at the end, but one that was repeated every day.

Hiroko would arrive in the morning, wearing jeans, chatting happily to her friends, giggling and chewing gum. She was an animated young woman who liked to laugh. But as soon as practice began, her face would be drained of all expression and become mask-like. Her voice would rise, and her bodily movements become as stylized as those of a Noh dancer.

At first, I must confess, I watched this spectacle with the

sniggering attitude of a typical Westerner, reaching for the clichéd image of Japanese as human robots. But Hiroko was very far from being a robot. Hers was a performance, and she took pride in it. I asked her in front of the camera why she had decided to become an elevator girl. She cocked her head and thought for a while, and then answered in one word: *akogare*. It is a word people use for something they yearn for, or dream about, as in *akogare no Paris,* Paris of our dreams. Young fans use precisely that word when they talk about the all-female Takarazuka theater.

The aesthetic of the human doll is of course the opposite of Kara Juro's idea of "the privilege of the flesh." The frenzy of his actors' bodily movements is a deliberate rebellion against the controlled beauty of the living bonsai that is part of the Japanese tradition. But his physical revolt, the dancing and fighting and face pulling and spitting and screaming onstage, is in fact just as much part of a Japanese tradition. It is the tradition of early Kabuki, the riverside beggars, the riotous Shinto festivals, the student demos in Shinjuku, and "the revolt of the body" in Hijikata's dance. Both traditions are stylized. They are two sides of the same aesthetic coin.

In 1978, a year after I translated *Mask of a Virgin,* Kara suddenly called me. He had something to tell me. I should come over right away. As I walked into the studio above Kara and Ri's house, some of the actors were smiling at me, as though they knew something I didn't. We sat down in a circle, as Kara explained the concept of his next play. It was to be called *Unicorn Monogatari, Tale of the Unicorn Taito-ku Version.*

Kara Juro in *Tale of the Unicorn*

Taito-ku was the name of the *shitamachi* ward where Kara was born. The play involved a labyrinth in Shitaya, his old neighborhood, and pork cutlets flying through the air, and a drag queen who raises a boy who was swapped in the Shitaya hospital for a girl, and a dog god, and men from a company dealing in baby swaddlers who fight over a plastic bag containing a placenta, and Sergeant Yokoi, the Imperial Army soldier who hid in the jungle of Guam until 1972, thinking the war was not yet over. The boy who was swapped in the Shitaya hospital as a baby was called Tessio, the Italian name for Theseus, and the girl was Adone, or Ariadne. And they drank each other's blood, and she would lead him through the labyrinth with a ball of thread, all the way to Narnia, the imaginary land in *The*

Kobayashi Kaoru carrying a placenta

Chronicles of Narnia by C. S. Lewis, while Tessio waved his wooden sword and pulled a bicycle with a unicorn's horn bolted to the handlebars.

I listened and nodded, and understood nothing. "And you," said Kara with a high-pitched chuckle, "you will be in the play. You will be Iwan the Gaijin, who might be a Russian but who claims to be the Midnight Cowboy."

NINE

Plot is perhaps not the main point of Kara's plays. I still don't really know what *Tale of the Unicorn* was all about. Rather than addressing the story directly, Kara talked around the play and its associations, which always came back to his childhood.

I asked him once whether he ever went to see Kabuki. The answer was that he didn't. No doubt, he said, "Kabuki is somewhere buried in my subconscious." His most vivid memories of theater were of quite another kind. He often recalled the striptease theaters in Asakusa, near his home in Shitaya. In between acts, to give the girls time to change into another scanty costume, comedians would do short sketches, comic swordfights, and the like, lasting no longer than five or ten minutes. Some of the punters, who had come to see the girls, would take that time to look over the horse racing results. But Kara was fascinated by these short bursts of slapstick between displays of naked flesh.

"Mitikin," Kara said in his excited half whisper, "at the Casino Theater. An alcoholic vaudevillian. He did the most amazing things. After locking swords with another comic onstage, Mitikin would rush out of the theater to the Asakusa temple, and rush back in again to resume the swordfight. I once visited him in his dressing room. He was munching rice crackers from a plastic bag. His shabby suit was covered in bits of cracker. And there were crackers all over the floor, too, which the girls crushed under their high heels. Suddenly Mitikin said: 'Listen! Do you hear the sound of a snowstorm in the forest?' "

This rather puzzling anecdote hinted at something important in the way Kara viewed the world: the shabby ambience of striptease theaters in Asakusa, the eccentricity of the sad old comedian, but above all the sudden switch from the literal to the simile, which often involves switches from low culture to high. The squalid absurdities of Kara's childhood world—the quarreling drag queens, the petty criminals, the sordid murder stories, the hookers—are woven into his own version of ancient myths: Ariadne helping Theseus to escape from the labyrinth in Tokyo *shitamachi,* looking for C. S. Lewis's Narnia. Characters, too, metamorphose in unexpected ways: the old drag queen, O-Haru, who swapped babies in the maternity hospital, suddenly pops up as Sergeant Yokoi, the man who hid from the world for twenty-eight years. Kara's plays unfold with the logic, or lack of logic, of dreams.

In short, there was nothing especially strange about my role as Iwan the Gaijin, who might be a Russian but claims to be the Midnight Cowboy.

My appearance in a ridiculous leather cowboy hat was quite short. In the third act, I was chased onto the stage by a marching band of the Narnia Volunteer Corps. The managing director of the baby swaddlers factory, who was also the dog god

Yatsufusa, played by Kobayashi Kaoru, called me a Russian. I said I wasn't a Russian. Who cares, he yelled, all white people look alike. Whereupon, pedantically, I tried to explain that the white race could be divided into Germanic people, or Slavic . . . Enough, shouted the dog god, from the point of view of the Peking Man, you're all bloody foreigners. You're a spy! Whereupon I cried out: "I am the Midnight Cowboy!" And so on it went for a while with more jokes about Russians, who had stolen Japanese territories in the Pacific after the war, and American GIs handing out chewing gum, a memory of which most people of Kara's age would retain from the postwar occupation.

The point was of course not to ridicule foreigners. The joke was on common Japanese attitudes to gaijin. I was immensely flattered to be in Kara's play. It made me feel accepted as one of the gang. Perhaps it even signified that I had some talent in the playwright's eyes. Here, at last, was real immersion in a small wet corner of Japanese society.

One night, after rehearsal, we went on one of those nocturnal excursions to Shinjuku. It was a balmy night in early spring, when the neon lights blinked like stars over streets that were dense and warm with traffic and crowds. We ended up in one of Kara's favorite haunts, a small bar popular with writers, called, if I remember well, Nadja, after André Breton's surrealist novel about a love affair with a madwoman. The lighting was low, the tables black, the room fogged with cigarette smoke. Miles Davis was playing softly in the background. It was a jolly evening. Bottles of whiskey were drained at a fast pace. I was seated next to Kara at his table, a place normally reserved for a senior member of the group. He looked every inch the boss, dressed in a powder-blue blazer and red silk tie, ordering more drinks all around, his eyes reduced to tiny slits, like a big contented cat. Most people called me by my first name, pronounced Iwan, as it was in the play. Someone said: "Iwan the Terrible." Someone else said: "Iwan the Gaijin." No, said a third person, "Iwan the Henna Gaijin," the weird foreigner; the foreigner, that is, who can speak Japanese, and who doesn't act like a stereotypical gaijin. I laughed, but I wasn't sure I liked the phrase. However well meant, it smacked a little of admiring a trained poodle for his adorable tricks.

Near the end of the evening, I found myself in the men's *room* standing next to Nezu, who played Tessio in *Tale of the Unicorn*. He turned his handsome Tokyo James Dean face toward me, while I was concentrating on the white porcelain wall, and said: "You know, you can only really act in our plays if you are a Japanese." I asked him what he meant. "Well," he said, "you can't act as a foreigner, if you are a gaijin."

I muttered something in disagreement. But his words stayed with me. I thought of the *onnagata* in Kabuki plays, the men specializing in female roles. Real women can't act these roles in the same stylized way. To get something of the flavor, women would have to play men playing women. I was a weird gaijin, supposed to play a Japanese acting as a foreigner. Perhaps that is what Nezu had meant to say. He may have been right. At least, that is how it felt to me sometimes.

Tale of the Unicorn would be performed in the red tent, of course. Our first stop on the tour was Osaka. The tent would be pitched on a grimy concreted hill in a park overlooking the city's main zoo. Then we would move on to a riverbank in Kumamoto, an old castle town on the southwestern island of Kyushu. And from there to Kyoto, and finally back to Tokyo, where we would perform on a sooty spot between the railway lines near Ikebukuro station. The whole run would last for almost a month.

Before we left, I was taken by one of the actors, Fuwa Mansaku, to meet the editor of the *Asahigraph,* the now defunct weekend supplement magazine of the *Asahi* newspaper. The idea was for me to take photographs of our tour and write an article about it. The editor, a lanky long-haired hipster-type in a dark gray suit, was very keen, he said, to get the "gaijin's view." He might even have used the common phrase used in media circles at the time, when a person like myself was commissioned to write something: "Japan seen through blue eyes."

I was overjoyed. Not only would I be one of the gang, but here was a chance to show that I had some talent, not only in my cameo appearance as the Midnight Cowboy, but as a writer and photographer. No longer just a film student, spy, or weird gaijin voyeur, but a person of substance, even if my eyes were not of the purest blue.

We set off early in the morning in a comfortable minibus, followed by a truck carrying the folded red tent. Kara and Ri were sitting near the front of the bus, chatting with Nezu, Kaoru, and other senior actors. We passed through the bland suburbs of Yokohama and the dusky green tea fields near Mount Fuji, whose cone was shrouded in fluffy white clouds. After a couple of hours, at some point between Toyohashi and Nagoya, I secluded myself in a window seat and started reading a book. I think it was a Dickens novel, *David Copperfield* perhaps. I liked reading such books on trips through Japan, or other parts of Asia: Jane Austen on a train to the northeast of Thailand, or Evelyn Waugh on a bus to the south of Taiwan. It was a way, I suppose, of escaping for a short while into an imaginary world that was reassuringly familiar.

I was woken from my immersion in David Copperfield's world of Steerforth and Mr. Micawber by a voice in my ear. It was the bucktoothed Fuwa Mansaku. "Why are you reading a book?" he asked. "You're not really used to traveling in a group, are you?" He did not say this unkindly, but it was a rebuke of sorts. One was supposed to join in, take part, share the experience of a common enterprise. To fall asleep on the bus was permissible, but reading a book was to shut oneself off from the others and clearly not done. I hastily put Uriah Heep and Betsey Trotwood out of my mind, and turned back to the real world of sitting with Kara and his players, drinking green tea from plastic containers, laughing at stories about old memories I could not share, and chewing on stringy bits of pale dried octopus on the highway to Osaka.

Tennoji Park, where we set up the tent after drilling holes in the rock-hard ground, is a remarkable spot. On one side is the zoo, so while rehearsing the story of a Japanese Theseus and Ariadne threading their way through Kara's native Shitaya in search of a lost mother's placenta carried in a gory plastic bag, we could hear the chattering of monkeys and the roar of a rather mangy lion moodily pacing up and down in his confinement.

On the other side of the park is an area called Shinsekai, or New World, a wonderfully seedy entertainment district, half nightlife area, half amusement park, built in 1912, inspired vaguely by a fantastical idea of New York and Paris. There is a broken-down Luna Park, a tower bearing a cursory resemblance to the Eiffel Tower, and rows of cheap restaurants specializing in plebeian delicacies such as grilled chicken gizzard and pig's heart. After World War II, the once-modern New World became a slum, run by the yakuza. Hoodlums in shiny suits and white patent-leather shoes swaggered through its narrow alleys, frightening respectable folks away. Down-and-outs came flocking from all over Japan to the skid row nearby, rather like Sanya in Tokyo, where the more robust men were handed out day jobs by yakuza contractors, if they were lucky; if not, they would get drunk on a cheap potato liquor called *shochu*. Along with the eateries offering grilled intestines, there were still some old music halls left, where washed-up comics wasted their tired jokes on a small number of snoring bums. The New World was also a magnet for drag queens and whores fishing for johns who were too drunk to bother about gender distinctions.

So here was a distinguished guest actor in our troupe, named Tokita Fujio, playing the part of O-Haru, the drag queen, made up in chalky white powder with a smear of lipstick across his mouth and a red rose stuck in his woolly black wig, while some of the creatures lolling about outside our tent looked far more extraordinary. There were middle-aged men in tattered long dresses. Some sported vinyl miniskirts, their scarred skinny legs tottering on stiletto heels. The female

Tokita Fujio as O-Haru, with Ri Reisen

prostitutes, too, were mostly on the elderly side, wearing similar getups to the men in drag.

I noticed a man slashing at bits of windswept paper with his blunted metal samurai sword. Someone told me that he fancied himself as Kunisada Chuji, a legendary nineteenth-century swordsman and gambler. No one spoke to him, and he ignored everyone around him, absorbed in his private dream world of outlaw derring-do. He was there every morning, and sometimes in the evenings, too, striking martial poses and cutting down imaginary enemies.

The dress rehearsal did not go well. Kaoru had a sore throat. Lines were fluffed. The pacing was wrong. Lighting cues were missed. Kara was nervous and made some of us rehearse our scenes again. But all was fine on the first night. My line about being the Midnight Cowboy got a huge cheer. "Feels good, doesn't it," Fuwa Mansaku whispered to me in the wings. But the biggest applause came at the end of the play, when the back of the tent opened up, revealing a red excavator truck with a power shovel that scooped up Tessio and O-Haru, while the music swelled and Tessio cried out: "Go, unicorn!"

It was, perhaps, the best performance of the tour. Before returning to the Buddhist temple, where we all slept on the large tatami floor in the main hall at the foot of gilded wooden bodhisattvas, we repaired to an old-fashioned public bathhouse, frequented mostly by tired men returning from the construction sites. On the wall was a splendid mosaic of the boy Kintaro riding an orange carp, a familiar image I had seen on Horibun's tattoos. We all shared the communal bath, of course, like rugby players immersed in the same scalding water, our red faces enveloped in steam. In the large temple hall, before laying out our futons, we drank copious amounts of beer, whiskey, and *shochu*. Kara did his rendition of "Ali Baba." Ri sang something from another play called *John Silver: Love in Shinjuku*. We all joined in, clapping hands. Nezu played the guitar. We had a friendly argument about the fate of the Palestinians. A toast was made to Iwan the Gaijin. All was well. Communal harmony seemed in perfect order.

And yet, there was a little fly in the ointment, a minor source of tension, which I had been slow to pick up on. Whenever Nezu appeared onstage, a large contingent of teenage girls in the audience started screaming deliriously. This was not the usual sound of appreciation in the red tent. It was more like the swelling shriek of a collective orgasm. At one point, Kara, in his role as the director of the hospital in Shitaya, told the girls to stop making so much noise, while shaking his bamboo stick at them. Rowdy audiences had always been part of the Situation Theater's neo-Kabuki style. Stars were used to being cheered. But the girls screaming at Nezu were not the usual Situation Theater fans. They were much younger. In fact, they were probably not really Situation Theater fans at all, but Nezu fans.

This might not have mattered so much if Nezu had acquired these fans as one of Kara's star actors. This was not the case, however. Shortly before going on tour with *Tale of the Unicorn*, Nezu had been cast in a popular television drama, playing a sixteenth-century outlaw named Ishikawa Goemon, a kind of Japanese Robin Hood. After a failed attempt to kill the most powerful warlord in Japan, Goemon was boiled alive in a cauldron, thus giving his name to a special kind of metal bathtub that is still in use. To enter this tub, one must be careful not to get scalded by the hot metal casing. In any case, Goemon is a glamorous figure, and the Tokyo James Dean was on his way to becoming a national heartthrob. Ri was starring in the same drama, and clearly had an appetite to do more television. Kara had a role in the show himself, but it was a minor part, as a pirate chief. He might have felt a certain wariness, and perhaps intimations of disloyalty. I didn't quite realize this at the time, when I was singing and clapping along at the Osaka temple, but I should have known something was amiss, when Kara, apropos of what I can't remember, said in a fit of peevishness: "Nezu, you're getting much too slick for your own good."

Nezu reacted by keeping his head down. But Ri was not the type to keep her head down. Her public rows with Kara were legendary in the small world of the Tokyo avant-garde. I had witnessed one or two of these explosions at their house. They were spectacular: Kara puffed up like an enraged bullfrog, Ri screaming her head off, tables of food being overturned. But I was assured that these episodes should be regarded as tokens of their passion for each other. They were like Stanley Kowalski and Stella in *A Streetcar Named Desire*. Confrontation was the spring of their creative juices. Kara's theater was unthinkable without the presence of Ri. And anyway, people said to me in private, Ri is Korean. Such outbursts are part of her Korean temperament.

Next stop Kumamoto. The tent was raised on the banks of

the Shirakawa River, in sight of Kumamoto Castle, a fine "old" building, constructed mostly in the sixteenth and seventeenth centuries, damaged in the civil war in the late nineteenth century, and reconstructed in concrete in the 1960s. As our mini-bus pulled up near the site, we could hear the by now familiar screeches and yelps from teenage girls in Mickey Mouse T-shirts and pink ankle socks. Kara yelled at them to get out of the way as we got off the bus. I, too, perhaps to ingratiate myself with Kara, and partly as a show of fitting in, voiced my annoyance with the teenage groupies. Nezu, disguised imperfectly by dark aviator glasses and a baseball cap, said to me, in English, "I'm sorry."

Riverbanks in Japan were the traditional haunts of outcasts, fairground entertainers, gamblers, petty thieves, traveling players, prostitutes, and other riffraff. The slummy outcast or *burakumin* areas are often still to be found along the less salubrious urban riverbanks. Hence the identification of Kara and his troupe with the "riverside beggars" who formed the first Kabuki troupes in the beginning of the seventeenth century.

The bank of the Shirakawa, where we were busily sticking tent poles into the muddy soil, was swarming with people. This time they were not drag queens or cheap hookers, but students banging on drums, playing trumpets, dancing, making out—in short, doing all the things for which there is little room or opportunity in the cramped confines of Japanese urban life. Two mannish-looking young women, with short-cropped hair and thick calves, strode up to our tent and introduced themselves as passionate Nezu fans. The couple looked like professional wrestlers. They told us they were employed as guards at a local women's prison. Kara was not terribly pleased to see them, but their friendliness and sheer oddness broke the ice. They handed out boxes of delicious homemade rice balls filled with cod roe and wrapped in blackish-green seaweed.

Kara, still in a grumpy mood, was doing his best to accommodate a local television reporter, a fat man in a white suit with chocolate-brown stripes, giving him a passing resemblance to an olive-skinned Fats Domino. But when asked to sum up the play in five minutes with a microphone held under his nose, Kara said no. I don't know how the interview proceeded after that, but about fifteen minutes later I spotted the fat man on his hands and knees barking at a stage prop of a dog. That was the last we saw of him.

The final rehearsal before our first performance in Kumamoto started late in the evening. Kara, in a soft leather jacket, stood in the murky reddish light of the tent in the hunched position of a boxer, his eyes fixed on the stage, silently mouthing the lines. Kaoru was still suffering from a sore throat. Rain was pelting down outside, creating a muddy delta around the tent, and making such a racket that it was hard to hear what was being said onstage. It was one o'clock in the morning by the time we were through, hoarse, hungry, and exhausted.

The following day one of Kara's oldest friends arrived on the scene, a cartoonist and manga artist named Akatsuka Fujio. His manga had become so famous that he was known as the Gag Manga King. Akatsuka had helped to finance the red tent. A pale, rather shy man, with a boyish fringe of black hair, born in Manchukuo the son of an officer in the dreaded military police, or Kempeitai, Akatsuka needed prodigious amounts of drink to unwind. Once he unwound, he was ready for anything. Araki, the photographer, had done a series of pictures of Aka-tsuka, dressed in a stripey T-shirt, fucking a young woman in a Shinjuku short-time hotel. To celebrate his visit to Kuma-moto, Kara cast him as one of the nurses in the Shitaya hospital. His entrance was rather spectacular, for he swam to the tent in the Shirakawa River, before emerging onstage in his drenched nurse's uniform. Perhaps it was the effect of the cold stream, but even though all he needed to do was stand onstage without saying anything, I had rarely seen anyone look so uncomfortable in the public gaze. He fidgeted about with a haunted look, desperate to dash back into the wings for a welcome glass of beer.

There were other famous visitors who came around after the performance. Miwa Akihiro was one, an actor and a cabaret singer. Miwa always dressed as a woman, onstage and off. He was reputed to have been Mishima's lover. They appeared together in the first film I ever saw in Japan, down in a small basement theater in Shinjuku. With a script written by Mishima himself, the movie, entitled *Kurotokage,* or *Black Lizard* (1969), is a perfect amalgam of homoerotic, sadomasochistic, Japanese–Oscar Wildean kitsch. Miwa plays the Black Lizard, a nightclub owner and criminal mastermind, a femme fatale oozing evil, who falls in love with the young detective working on her case. Mishima appears in the film as a buff gangster (all his body-building efforts on full display), who is murdered by the Black Lizard and turned into a nude sculpture for her to play with in her nightclub. Astonishingly, this morbid fantasy was first produced as a musical in 1962. Mishima, apparently, preferred the later version starring Miwa.

Miwa spoke highly effeminate Japanese in a growling masculine voice. He claimed to be the incarnation of a pretty adolescent boy who led a seventeenth-century rebellion by Christian
peasants against the samurai rulers in southern Kyushu. The
rebellion ended with a massacre of all the local Christians. The
boy's head was displayed on a pike in Nagasaki, Miwa's native
town. I had been introduced to Miwa once before, in a Ginza
nightclub where he sang French chansons à la Edith Piaf. I
found him rather terrifying.

The reaction of such visitors to my presence was usually
something like: "My, my, look at how international the Situation Theater has become these days." Sometimes, too, I would
be pumped with questions about life in the United States, as if
I knew. Under sufficient provocation, I would respond by putting on my supercilious Japanese act to the point, almost, of
imitating Kara's *shitamachi* accent. I must have been insuffer-
able, not to say inscrutable. But in fact, none of these remarks
by the distinguished visitors were meant to provoke. I suppose
what irked me was the reminder of my uncertain status in the
group: one of the gang, privileged gaijin, international mascot,
or spy?

Perhaps it was the presence of Miwa that affected my concentration. But the second night in Kumamoto was a minor
disaster. I got to the bit about being the Midnight Cowboy all
right, but then suddenly my mind blanked. I saw Kaoru wait
for my next line, with a slight nervous twitch in the corner of
his mouth. Panic struck, my throat went dry, sweat stung in my
eyes, and I could sense the audience wondering what was
wrong. It was like being sucked into a void. The harder my

heart thumped in my chest, the more the words escaped me. I did not have the professional skill to cover up and improvise until I calmed down. After long, endless, mortifying seconds had gone by, Kaoru audibly fed me my next line. It didn't happen again, but it was petrifying while it lasted. And worse, Kara was deeply annoyed.

We left Kumamoto in the minibus at dawn. Mist still clung to the road like shreds of gauze. Minutes later, we left the minor road to enter the highway heading north. There, on the corner, stood the two female prison guards, frantically waving their handkerchiefs. God knows how long they had been waiting to catch a glimpse of us (or Nezu) in the early morning. Most of us waved back.

The riverbed of the Kamogawa in Kyoto is, in a way, a hallowed space, for that is where the Kabuki theater began. Around 1603, a former Shinto shrine dancer named Izumo no Okuni gathered a number of outcasts and prostitutes to form an all-female acting troupe. They danced on the dry riverbed and performed sketches of love trysts in the Kyoto brothels. The style caught on, not least in the pleasure quarter itself. A decade or so later, the authorities, in one of their periodic efforts to crack down on public lewdness and uncontrolled prostitution, banned performances by female actors. So young men took over and played the female roles. Apparently this did nothing to diminish the appetite for paying actors to have sex. So in due course, young men were banned from the stage as well, unless they shaved their pates in the adult fashion. And thus a great theatrical tradition was born that continues in a somewhat fossilized state today. One of the most moving performances I have ever seen in any theater was in Osaka, of a famous scene where a young samurai is forced to sell his wife to a brothel in Kyoto to raise money for a vendetta against a wicked courtier who had forced the young man's lord to slit his belly. An up-and-coming actor played the role of the young samurai. His own father, the venerable Nakamura Ganjiro, then in his eighties, played his young wife. But I suppose this was no stranger than seeing Montserrat Caballé, also in Osaka, a few years later, sing Tosca when she was far too bulky to jump off the wall that was no higher than a shoebox.

There, more or less on the same spot where Izumo no Okuni once danced, the red tent went up for the final performances before returning to Tokyo. We stayed in the same old student dorm where I had been with Maro's Dairakudakan troupe. On the night before the opening show, Kara along with some of the main players and myself, ever the privileged gaijin, were taken out for dinner in Ponto-cho, an ancient district of cobbled streets and narrow alleys where Kyoto geisha flit in and out of graceful wooden and bamboo "teahouses." On the riverbank there is now a rather hideous statue of a very respectable, even demure-looking Okuni, doing a kind of sword dance. Our host was a well-known surrealist poet, whose name now escapes me.

We sat in a row at the cypress wood counter of an exclusive Japanese restaurant, where the raw fish was so fresh that some morsels were still twitching on the pretty porcelain dishes. One man, not in our group, was poking a trembling prawn with his chopstick. The prawn was dead, and could not have suffered, but there was an element of sadism about the scene that still sticks in my mind. The discussion on surrealism in Japan was fascinating and well over my head. Kara talked about André Breton, and about Nagai Kafu, the literary flaneur and keen visitor of Asakusa strip theaters, who was found dead in his study with breadcrumbs all over his suit. At some point in the evening, I thought it would be amusing to tell the distinguished poet about our encounters with Nezu's screaming devotees. This was followed by an unamused silence. I asked Kaoru later whether I had made a gaffe. "Well," he said, "we all know what you said was true, but we don't necessarily have to spell it out, do we?"

Our final performance in Kyoto was a triumph. It was a warm night. The Kamogawa shimmering with reflected neon lights never looked more beautiful. The audience was loud and appreciative, and the hard-core Nezu fans were not much in evidence. After we had scrubbed off our makeup, Ri left us to have dinner with a friend somewhere in town. The rest of us followed Kara into the minibus to celebrate our last night in an old Kyoto restaurant, where sword marks from boisterous nineteenth-century samurai could still be seen on the blackened wood of the entrance hall. A sumptuous dinner of traditional Kyoto cuisine was waiting for us in a large room on the second floor, where we sat down on silk cushions on an olive-colored tatami floor. In one corner of the room was a scroll painting of a Zen monk suspended above a lovely iris flower arrangement.

This time, we had another guest in our midst. I recognized him instantly as a minor star in the yakuza movies. His name was Kawatani Takuzo, whose main role in gangster pictures was to pull fearsome faces and die, always in a violent manner, rather early on in the story. Kawatani was in fact a ham, cast more for his peculiar looks than his acting skills. His eyebrows met in a thick black line across his shifty little eyes, lending an air of dumb brutality to a man who seemed perfectly amiable offscreen. He had come to see our play out of deference to Ri. They had starred together in a successful TV drama.

I wasn't paying much attention to Kawatani, who was sitting next to Kara. I was at the other end of a long table. It is possible that Kawatani had already had a few drinks before we arrived at the restaurant, but he didn't look particularly the worse for wear. But soon I sensed the beginning of an altercation with Kara. I wasn't close enough to see what started it. Later, I was told that Kawatani had been needling Kara in a particularly sore spot. The theater was old hat, he supposedly claimed. Kara was wasting his time. He should be doing more television or movies, like Ri. And so, apparently, it went on for a while, until Kara suddenly made his move. He lurched toward his guest. The gangster actor's face was drenched in beer, and Kara started furiously pummeling him with his fists. This was the sign for others to join the fray. For a short while, Kawatani was buried under a group of actors showing their solidarity by furiously pounding the small writhing figure on the tatami, lightly sprinkled by splashes of blood. Once he emerged from the scrum, it was clear that Kawatani's face was a mess. A phone call was quickly made, and he was removed from the premises on a stretcher.

I was speechless, as usual in scenes of actual violence. More than anything, it was the mob behavior of my fellow actors that shook me. Once again I felt I was out of step with the group, like when I was absorbed in *David Copperfield* on the way to Osaka. I can't remember what was said after the fight. The evening is a blank until an hour or so later, when Ri finally turned up. She had heard what had happened and was in a howling rage. Standing in the middle of the room, she wagged her finger at Kara, who was still sitting on the floor, and started screaming at him. What did he think he was doing? How dare he attack her friend and colleague in this manner? Who did he think he was?

Kara's face went a darker red. He cursed his wife, grabbed a heavy ashtray, like a glass brick, and flung it at her. Missing her head by inches, the ashtray shattered the wall covered in elegant rice-paper paneling.

I was so stunned that I didn't really know what I was doing. But I remember getting to my feet and blurting out to Kara something absurd like: "You can't do that to a woman!" There was a moment of baffled silence around the room. Kara could not believe what he was hearing. His furious eyes swiveled in my direction. His voice dropped to a menacing growl, like a dangerous animal under threat: "How dare you speak to me like that!"

I still don't know why I did it. What possessed me to humiliate Kara in this way in front of his actors? I should have known better than to interfere in a fight between husband and wife. What was behind this pompous gesture of chivalry? Could it have had something to do with my shaky sense of self in the midst of a Japanese theater troupe? Was it a displaced cry to be seen for who I really was? Did I even know myself?

But I shall never forget Kara's words, repeated in unabated anger in the bus on our way back to the dormitory: "So you are just an ordinary gaijin after all!"

TEN

Ah," said Kara with a crooked smile, "I can see the whities already." He used the word *keto,* literally hairy foreigner, a derogatory term used only for white people, even though the *to* refers to China, which in the olden days stood for the outside world.

Kara was in a cheerful mood. We were entering one of the terminals of the brand-new Narita International Airport, still surrounded by high fences, numerous checkpoints, and thousands of security police milling around among Japanese and *keto* checking in. The construction of Narita on expropriated village land had been the last focal point of Japanese mass protest in the twentieth century. Before Narita was officially opened, left-wing protesters had managed to take over the control tower. Six thousand demonstrators tried to disrupt the official opening. A Japanese newscaster compared the place to the Saigon airport during the Vietnam War.

We were soon to be on our way to New York, the first time Kara and Ri would set foot in a Western country.

This was in the late summer of 1978, about three months

after the ashtray-throwing incident in Kyoto. It had not been an easy time. Kara was still smarting from my insulting behavior. My enthusiasm for performing Iwan the Gaijin was waning. But we were still roped together, as the Tokyo leg of the tour had to be completed. The tent was set up near the railway siding in Ikebukuro. We played to full houses on most nights.

Relations did not improve when my article about our adventures with the Situation Theater appeared in the *Asahi* magazine. They had given it a good spread. I thought my color photographs looked fine. I had written what I thought was a friendly piece about the effect of a traveling theater troupe on its surroundings, how the red tent created an atmosphere of drama wherever it was pitched. I described the female prison wardens in Kumamoto and the swordsman in Osaka. I mentioned Kara's tense encounters with Nezu's screaming fans. I had reached for a tone that was sympathetic and, I thought, funny. But I'm afraid it was not received in that spirit. On the contrary it further fanned the flames of Kara's rage.

Perhaps this was partly a matter of language. Irony does not translate well into Japanese. It can easily come across as sarcasm. But I think something else was the matter too. I had failed to write as an insider. Having been offered the chance to take my place in the gang as an honorary member, I had described the troupe with an air of detachment. This distancing was perhaps regarded as hostile. I had learned an important lesson about writing. When you turn friends into characters or figures in a landscape, you run the danger of causing offense, because the way you see them, however well intentioned, may not be the way they see themselves. And who wants to be a figure in a landscape anyway? I think that was at least part of the problem. Kara never gave me a detailed critique. All he said, after a long and angry sulk, was: "Iwan, you are"—and here he used the English phrase—"a cynical guy."

Still, all seemed to be forgotten near the end of the season, when the famous Romanian-American theater director Andrei Serban turned up in the tent one night. Serban, a tall, blond, somewhat Christ-like figure, had left his native Bucharest in 1969 for New York. He had directed a controversial *Medea* at Ellen Stewart's La MaMa Experimental Theatre Club. Later he did a number of Chekhov plays starring Meryl Streep and F. Murray Abraham, upsetting some conventional critics with his idiosyncratic interpretations. He once said that Broadway producers wouldn't go near him, since he was known as "the director who destroys the classics."

Serban was thrilled by *Tale of the Unicorn*. "It is like Commedia dell'arte!" he exclaimed after the performance, back in Kara's studio. "It is like Kabuki! It is the essence of theater!" I translated. Kara was all smiles, making sure our glasses of whiskey were kept full. Serban told Kara he *had* to come to New York. People there had never seen anything like the Situation Theater. They would love it. Kara's eyes took on a dreamy expression. "To put up the tent in Central Park, now that would really be something." Yes, cried Serban, "Central Park, the red tent will arise in Central Park!"

And that is how we ended up at Narita International Airport bound for New York. I don't know how much Andrei Serban had to do with the organization. Various foundations and cultural councils had been involved. I was to accompany Kara and Ri as their translator and guide. Mine was not a paid job, but more something done in the spirit of friendship; this is the way many things worked in Japan; mutual obligations are built up over time and not always expressed in cash. I had been to New York only once before in my life, but I was happy to "guide" my Japanese friends in the *keto* labyrinth.

Kara peered into the night from the airplane window as New York City twinkled below us like a vast blanket of fairy lights, turned his head away in a gesture of disdain, and said: "Seoul is really much more impressive, isn't it."

I had booked us into the Chelsea Hotel because I had read in some magazine that it was a hip place to be. Andy Warhol had shot a movie there. Jane Fonda and Jimi Hendrix had been residents. When we checked in, a painfully thin man in a tattered black top hat and a white woman's petticoat was nodding off in the lobby. The rooms were so seedy that fat slugs left slimy traces on the stained carpets full of cigarette burns. A reek of marijuana and bad plumbing hung in the halls. I thought this would be the perfect place to start Kara's journey to the West. In a memoir, written some years later, Kara described the hotel as *ikagawashii,* meaning dubious, suspicious, or unseemly.

The reason for coming to New York was of course to meet people and see plays. My memory of the meetings is now a blur. I do recall Ellen Stewart at La MaMa. Her splendid cornrows had not yet gone silver. It was a hot Saturday afternoon in the East Village. A block party had turned the street over to a mass of people dancing to the sounds of Bob Marley. She told us how the whole world was coming together right there in the Village.

They had staged a Korean *Hamlet* at La MaMa a year before. "Child," Stewart said, "if a play beeps to me, I'll put it on." The array of armbands and bracelets that ringed her thin brown arms made a pleasant clinking sound as she sashayed her way down the block, greeting neighbors like the queen of East Fourth Street.

We saw Joe Papp at the Public Theater, who, after being introduced to Kara Juro and Ri Reisen of the Red Tent Theater, greeted them as Mr. and Mrs. Red Tent. Even though Kara had criticized me the night before for not translating every word that a man from the Rockefeller Foundation had spoken, I decided that Papp's condescension could do without a translation. Papp looked preoccupied, sitting behind his desk, with frequent glances at his watch. Well, he said, yes, a theater tent in Central Park, yes that sure could be interesting.

We saw the incomparable Charles Ludlam perform in an impossibly camp version of *The Lady of the Camellias* (he acted as the Lady, of course) in a tiny former gay nightclub on Sheridan Square.

We went to Central Park to see Meryl Streep and Raúl Juliá perform in *The Taming of the Shrew*. Andrei Serban was with us, bubbling with enthusiasm. Keep an eye on that young Streep, he said, she's going to be a big star.

We even went up to a disused parking lot in Harlem one night, where a group of "socially engaged" black actors were entertaining the neighborhood people for free. We were told by whoever it was that sent us up there which streets to avoid. Harlem was still an edgy place back then.

I can't remember what else we saw. But Kara and Ri were remarkably blasé about the theater in New York. Even

Ludlam's wild antics left them rather cold. I think they found American acting too cerebral, not physical enough. Ri observed that Americans didn't "act with their lower bodies." An aspiring young performer belting out a show tune to the crowd queuing up in front of a Broadway theater left a greater impression on them than Streep, Ludlam, or Juliá.

Kara in particular appeared not to be excited by anything much. He was oddly incurious about a city he had never visited before. When Ri suggested going to one of the great museums, Kara said rather curtly that he would stay in the hotel. "Do you really think," he said, "Andrei Serban would be going to museums in Tokyo?"

One thing Kara did observe was something that would not have surprised any New Yorkers. The streets were full of panhandlers at the time; ragged people sprawled on park benches; or emaciated junkies in subway tunnels or in the lobbies of crumbling apartment buildings. What struck Kara, however, was not the number of down-and-outs, but the fact that so many of them were white. The sight of a poor, begging *keto* was an anomaly to him, something almost against nature. He expressed no satisfaction in this, just a sense of wonderment.

A year before, in the Summer of Sam, a serial killer, claiming to have heard the voice of a demon dog in his head, had gunned down strangers at random in the outer boroughs of New York. I can't remember who suggested going on a tour of the murder sites, but there we were in a taxi, prowling obscure bits of Queens and the Bronx, with the knowledgeable cab driver filling us in on the precise details of the killings.

Mostly, however, Kara stayed in the hotel, writing his next

play, while Ri and I went for walks or to the movies. We saw Faye Dunaway in a mediocre picture called *Eyes of Laura Mars* playing a fashion photographer being stalked in New York by a serial killer. Kara's decision to shut himself off in his hotel room might have been a form of posturing; an effort to do as he thought Andrei Serban would have done in Japan. Or perhaps it was a form of shyness.

. I had read accounts of other famous Japanese artists and writers who reacted defensively to being in a strange Western city unrecognized among strangers. Sudden obscurity could be painful to grand men who were used to deference, even adulation, at home. Mishima, I had been told, found this particularly irksome. He spent his first time in New York in an almost constant huff. Indifference was sometimes rather too quickly interpreted as racial prejudice.

In 1965, Oe Kenzaburo, who would later win the Nobel Prize for literature, sent a postcard to his translator from New York: "A few days ago I was introduced to Norman Mailer at a bar late at night. He ignored me as if I were a small dog, or maybe a visiting dentist from an undeveloped country. Alas!"*

The pride of local fame, however, is not the only possible explanation. The great Natsume Soseki almost went mad with solitude during his two years of studying in London. He wrote about that unhappy time, much of it spent in the seclusion of his lodgings in South London: "Everyone I see on the street is tall and good-looking. That, first of all intimidates me, embarrasses

---

* Quoted in John Nathan's memoir, *Living Carelessly in Tokyo and Elsewhere*, New York: Free Press, 2008.

me. Sometimes I see an unusually short man, but he is still two inches taller than I am . . . Then I see a dwarf coming, a man with an unpleasant complexion—and he happens to be my own reflection in the shop window."* But this was in 1903, some years before Soseki became the most famous novelist in Japan.

Then there is the so-called Paris syndrome, a phrase coined by the press at the end of the twentieth century to describe Japanese tourists whose first encounter with Paris (or any other Western city idealized from afar) made them go slightly mad, so they would have to be repatriated. Something like that happened to a pale, bookish Japanese student called Sagawa Issei, who spent almost four years studying French without much success. In the early summer of 1981, he lured a beautiful Dutch student called Renée Hartevelt, who spoke fluent French, to his apartment with an excuse about wanting her to read a German poem.

Sagawa, then thirty-two years old, had a peculiar history with white women. He had assaulted a German woman in Tokyo ten years before. Something he wrote about his life in Paris echoed Soseki's sentiments in a strange way. Sitting in a café one day: "Suddenly I looked at the glass front door of the café and reflected there were the five of us. A small Oriental in a charcoal blazer was submerged amid large white-skinned men and women. Instinctively I looked away."†

On that ill-fated day in June, in Sagawa's apartment, Renée Hartevelt turned around to read the German poem, and Sagawa shot her in the back with a rifle. He raped her corpse, sliced her

---

* Quoted in Masao Miyoshi, *Accomplices of Silence: The Modern Japanese Novel*, Berkeley: University of California Press, 1974.
† Sagawa Issei, *Kiri no Naka* (*In the Fog*), Tokyo: Hanashi no Tokushu, 1983.

up in pieces, ate some parts, and kept some in his refrigerator, before packing up the remains in a suitcase, which he tried to dump in the Bois de Boulogne, alas for him, in full sight of some French cops. While locked up in a French mental institution, Sagawa became a kind of cult antihero in Japan, where writers and intellectuals wrote about him with an appalled (and often appalling) fascination for the ultimate taboo-breaking sex crime.

Unwilling to keep him any longer, the French authorities sent Sagawa back to Japan a few years later, where he was examined in a mental hospital and declared sane. Since he had never been officially convicted, he was now free to appear on television talk shows, and even play a small part as a sex murderer in a porno movie.

Oshima Nagisa was interested in making a film about the case. And so was Kara. Nothing came of these plans. But Kara wrote a novel in 1982, entitled *Letters from Sagawa,* about his semifictional attempt to meet the killer in Paris. It was a morbidly playful book, full of references to *keto,* to the impossibility of translation, and to the neurotic attitudes of Japanese toward white foreigners: "That 'yearning' for the skin of 'white' people which for long years tormented and drove you on is not something I, who have myself been looked-down upon by women of foreign parts, cannot understand."* In 1983, Kara won the most prestigious Japanese literary prize for his book.

To interpret Kara's behavior in New York in hindsight through the lens of his strange novel would be unfair. I saw no

---

* The translation is by Mark Morris, from whose article "The Question of the Other: Kara Juro and *Letters from Sagawa,*" in *The Asia-Pacific Journal,* vol. 5, no. 12 (December 2007), I have borrowed much of this information.

evidence that Kara's amour propre was bruised by New York. But he did write some years later that the American trip had made him reflect more deeply on his own background. He felt the need to "maintain the balance" of his Japaneseness by writing a play, called *Kappa,* full of references to the muddiest aspects of Japanese culture. The *kappa* is a sprite in Japanese myths, a demonic trickster lurking in rivers and lakes. But the *kappa* in Kara's play is the reincarnation of a drowned boy living in a tatami room that turns into a bog. And so it goes on, deep into Kara's fantasy world, taking him away from unfamiliar New York back to the swampy soil of Tokyo.

Our return flight to Japan was canceled for a reason I have forgotten, something to do with the weather perhaps. So we had to make a stop in San Francisco, where we spent the day wandering around rather listlessly. After Ri returned to the hotel for a rest, Kara and I ended up in a run-down old theater in Chinatown. We arrived in the middle of a crude and very noisy Cantonese opera. Next to us, an old man was snoring through the crashing, banging, and wailing sounds onstage. Others cleared their throats and spat on the floor just as a young nobleman was declaring his love to a courtesan. We were the only non-Chinese, so far as I could make out. And I was the only *keto*. I followed Kara's gaze, as I had been doing metaphorically all through our trip; I wanted to see what he saw. Kara was less interested in the stage action than in the ambience, the colored lights beaming in from the back of the theater, the comings and goings of the musicians. It was the first time that week that I had seen him looking entirely relaxed.

After a meal of Chinese noodles, we walked into a random

dimly lit bar. A rather hideous bunch of dusty plastic flowers was arranged on the bar top. Next to it was a large golden cat, also made of plastic, lazily waving one paw up and down when you nudged it. An old airline poster of Mount Fuji hung on the wall. Behind the bar was an Asian woman, probably in her midsixties, heavily made up, with frizzy reddish-dyed hair tied into a knot with a pink chiffon scarf.

Kara whispered in my ear: "What does she remind you of?" I had read enough about modern Japanese history to know the answer: "A *pan pan* girl." Yes, giggled Kara, in high excitement. *Pan pan* girls were Japanese prostitutes who plied the bombed-out ruins of Tokyo for customers just after the war. Some specialized in Japanese men, some accepted Koreans and Chinese, too; some went only for the *keto* in uniform, and some only for black GIs.

Hearing us speak in Japanese, the bar lady stretched her crimson lips in a broad smile, exposing a row of cigarette-stained teeth. Her story followed quickly. She had come to the United States in the late 1940s with her American husband, a navy man. They soon got divorced. Ever since, she had been working in one bar or another. But business was no longer what it once was. Her looks, her manner of speaking, her rural Japanese accent, all spoke of a different time, when Kara grew up in the low city and GIs swaggered around Tokyo in their jeeps. She could have been one of the women living among the drag queens in a public lavatory on Kara's street in 1946. Time had stood still for her, as it often does for lifelong expatriates, who become almost like caricatures of their younger selves. I had seen examples of this among the gaijin expatriates in Tokyo;

they become professional Englishmen or Americans, hold more and more reactionary political opinions, and drink too much.

"So what are you going to do with your life?" Kara asked me after our third *mizuwari*. It was not a question I could answer with any conviction, so I mumbled something about being a photographer. "Yes, yes, photography," he said rather dismissively, "but we believed in your talent. How old are you now? You'd better get a move on, you know. I set up our first red tent in Shinjuku when I was still in my twenties."

The bar lady had been playing a succession of songs by Charles Aznavour. She liked French chansons, she told us, especially Aznavour-san. Americans don't understand French songs, she said, unlike us Japanese. She patted her heart, and said: "Feeling. The same feeling." Kara nodded: "Exactly so." Edith Piaf sang "Milord." The bar lady emerged from her perch behind the bar and began to dance, fluttering her thin hands in the air like a twenties flapper. She asked me to dance with her. Kara got all excited, turned around on his bar stool, clapping his hands, his high-pitched voice rising above Piaf's: "Yes, Iwan, dance with her! Dance! Dance!"

And I danced.

ELEVEN

I did not see much of Kara after we returned to Tokyo. My honorary position in the Situation Theater had come to an end.

Kara was right, of course: I was just an ordinary gaijin after all. It was as though I had flunked an important test; my immersion in a Japanese gang had run into an insurmountable barrier. That last night in Kyoto had been the moment of truth that all foreigners face in Japan at one point or another. No matter how much you might behave as a Japanese, you never will be Japanese. Some foreigners find this painful. But you cannot blame the Japanese for failing to comply with the illusions of foreigners. Just as Kara faced his Japaneseness in the Chelsea Hotel, every gaijin in Japan must realize that a gaijin he or she will always remain, no matter how well a person speaks Japanese or has mastered the etiquette of Japanese social life.

One of the finest descriptions of a Westerner's disillusion in Asia comes at the end of E. M. Forster's novel *A Passage to India*. Mr. Fielding, the free-spirited English professor, wants to revive his friendship with Dr. Aziz, the Indian Muslim who was deeply wronged by the false accusation of molesting an Englishwoman. Fielding had supported his friend all through his ordeal. He respected the Indians, Muslims as well as Hindus, and tried hard to understand their cultures. He came close to "going native," that great colonial taboo. But the resumption of his friendship with Dr. Aziz is not to be, not yet, not there, in British India. Fielding asks: "Why can't we be friends . . . It's what I want. It's what you want." But, Forster writes in the last paragraph, "the horses didn't want it—they swerved apart; the earth didn't want it, sending up rocks through which riders must pass single file."

Forster was not convinced that East and West could never meet. "Only connect" remained his hope for overcoming differences of culture and religion. The rocks in his final metaphor were thrown up, not by cultural difference, but by the colonial system, which prevented even the best meaning of men like Fielding and Aziz from being equals. This leaves the door open for future change; Aziz can still promise the Englishman that after the British have been thrown out of India, "you and I shall be friends."

An element of this plays a role in the gaijin's relation to Japan, even though Japan was never colonized—occupied, yes, briefly by the Allied forces led by the Americans, but not colonized. Nevertheless, when I lived in Tokyo, the white foreigner stood too far outside the norms of Japanese society to be treated as an equal. There had been too much history of assumed white superiority. Japanese nerves were still sometimes raw. On rare occasions, the gaijin might be the subject of hatred or contempt. More often, he was privileged. I was not treated by Kara as I would have been had I been a stagestruck Japanese of my age. In a sense, the gaijin is offered a sojourn in a fool's paradise. For some lucky fools the sojourn might stretch to a lifetime.

Kara occasionally mentioned John Nathan, an American who had preceded me in the social thickets of Japanese film, theater, and literature. Nathan lived in Tokyo in the glorious 1960s, where he had distinguished himself far more than I ever had. He appeared in major plays, wrote the script for a movie starring Ri Reisen, and translated Mishima. Nathan was the first American to be admitted as a regular student of Japanese literature at Tokyo University, where he had "felt the exhilaration of belonging to the group. I felt Japanese."*

But not for long. A famous Japanese movie star named Katsu Shintaro, celebrated for his performance as Zatoichi, the blind samurai swordsman, told John that he understood the Japanese like no other foreigner, that he spoke Japanese like a native, but, John, he said, *"in Japan you cannot win!"* What he meant was that foreigners would never be judged by the same rules. For years, Nathan wrote in his memoir, "I had been troubled by the possibility that I possessed the wherewithal to distinguish myself only as an exotic foreigner in an insular island country. I determined to prove myself on home ground."

I had learned a similar lesson, which Kara, wittingly or not, had taught me. But there is an important difference between the gaijin's experience in Japan and that of Mr. Fielding in colonial India, or Kara's in New York City. And this is something Forster does not touch upon, at least not overtly. Kara's

---

* *Living Carelessly in Tokyo and Elsewhere*, New York: Free Press, 2008.

Japaneseness is defined by the culture of his native country. Fielding and Aziz are drawn apart by colonial inequality. But the exotic white foreigner in Japan remains fixed forever to a racial or ethnic type. These differences can be exaggerated, of course. Race, social inequality, and history overlap. To many Japanese, perhaps most, to be Japanese *is* an ethnic category, like a birthmark that can never be erased. I once had a conversation with Kara about the plight of the outcasts in Japan, the *burakumin,* who are condemned by birth in *buraku* families to be marked forever by their ancestral association with death, even if they are dentists or schoolteachers instead of butchers or tanners. Kara then said something extraordinary: "You know, I think of the whole of Japan as a *buraku.*" The notion of the Japanese as outcasts in the world seems patently absurd, redolent of an unpleasant sense of self-pity. And yet Kara put his finger on something real: the difference between outcasts and a chosen people, driven by quasi-religious propaganda in the 1930s and early '40s to dominate Asia as the descendants of the sun goddess, is not so great. But that precisely was the rock that separated the Japanese, not as individuals, but as a people, from others. That is why I, like John Nathan, decided I needed to leave.

It is of course perfectly possible for a foreigner to lead a contented and productive life in Japan. There are various ways of coming to terms with the gaijin status, some more enervating than others. One can simply enjoy the privileges without the illusion of ever being anything but an outsider. In some ways, that is the easiest option most likely to lead to a kind of serenity. Not speaking Japanese very well, or at all, can be reassuring to

222

the native born. There is no pretense, no performance, no attempt at passing; the foreigner is precisely what he appears to be. The inscrutability of the Oriental is an old colonial prejudice. But it is also something to which many Japanese cling. To remain beyond the understanding of outsiders confirms the uniqueness of the native culture.

This insularity can be a source of constant irritation to some foreigners who try their best to understand; the Mr. Fieldings who would have liked to have gone native, in one way or another. Even if the irritation is not constant, it can recur often enough to become like a neurotic compulsion. Edward Seidensticker, the great American scholar and translator of Japanese, lived in Tokyo for several years in the 1960s, when he wrote a sometimes acid but always amusing column for the English edition of a large Japanese newspaper. He wrote an extraordinary valedictory column, published in May 1962, where he explained his reasons for leaving Japan to return to the United States.

There once was a meadow mouse, he writes, who was thought to be unreasonable on the subject of a fat snake slithering around outside the meadow mouse's hole. The snake bore a striking resemblance to certain Japanese politicians and bureaucrats. A friendly fellow mouse tells him to relax, have another drink, and just make friends with the snake. Snakes, after all, are just like other folks: they work hard to support their children, they enjoy baseball, and so on. The meadow mouse, getting drunker all the time, is finally convinced by his friend, lets down his guard, and is swiftly devoured by the snake in one satisfied gulp.

But not Professor Seidensticker: "I have felt recently that I might be getting mellow, becoming a reasonable meadow mouse. The Japanese are just like other people. They work hard to support their—but no. They are not like other people. They are infinitely more clannish, insular, parochial, and one owes it to one's self-respect to preserve a feeling of outrage at the insularity. To have the sense of outrage go dull is to lose the will to communicate; and that, I think, is death. So I am going home."*

Remember, this was written in 1962. The fat snake metaphor is a rather dubious one. And much has changed since then. But perhaps not as much as sufferers of gaijinitis might wish. The arguments between the meadow mouse and his friend are still being fought out in the letter columns of the English-language press in Japan, where outraged complaints about Japanese insularity are countered by assertions that Japan is misunderstood, that Japanese are just like other people, or indeed in most respects superior to other people. If the foreigner in Japan is a writer, these arguments can become the main focus of his work, an obsessive theme that will not go away, an endless debate that neither side can win. For an insular people can also be misunderstood, clannish people can still be like other people, and some foreigners will find living in Japanese society more congenial than others.

Those who find it most congenial often make a virtue of their outsider status, embracing their gaijinhood like a protective shell. This is rather like going native, paradoxical as this may sound. For living in a society, to whose customs and norms

---

* Reprinted in *This Country, Japan,* Tokyo: Kodansha International, 1979.

one is not expected to conform, gives the outsider a radical kind of autonomy. But the point of this is not to rebel against the norms of the country one has chosen to live in, but of those one has left behind. This is what Donald Richie was trying to tell me when we were first introduced by John Roderick, the American newspaperman, in the apartment of their friend, the gay British novelist.

The Richie solution is now less common in Japan than it once was. Western gay men have less reason to fear the customs and norms of their own societies, and gaijin don't enjoy the same radical autonomy they once did. Strangers are no longer quite so strange in Japan. Along with prejudice against gaijin, their privileges have shrunk. More and more, residents of Japan are expected to do as the Japanese do. And this is the way it ought to be.

And yet, the voice of the meadow mouse cannot be stilled entirely. Despite the extraordinary spread of certain aspects of Japanese culture—sushi, manga, Pokémon —Japan still is an insular nation, not much understood in the rest of the world. This opens up great opportunities to a writer, who knows Japan even a little bit, for so much still needs to be explained. I benefited from this myself. It was the start of my life as a journalist. Not long after my trip to New York with Kara and Ri, I was asked by a British newspaper to fill an entire issue of their Sunday magazine with articles on Japan, illustrated by my own photographs. This led to a contract for my first book. Japan was the making of me.

And yet I didn't want to spend all my writing life explaining Japan. The constant explainer runs the risk of no longer learning, and becoming a bore. And I didn't feel the same need to escape that shaped the life of my great American mentor. I had no reason to fear the customs and norms of my own culture. What I did fear was to catch a dose of gaijinitis, and become obsessed with the often imaginary slights that go with being pegged to one's ethnicity.

And so I said goodbye to Japan. But not to go home. I was no longer sure where home was. Holland, where I grew up, did not really feel like home. London, where my English mother grew up, was as good a place as any. Not because I could ever feel entirely English myself. That, too, was a performance to an extent. But I chose London because I wanted to live among people who could read what I wrote in their own language, a language I was not educated in but was still part of me. Because of my mother, I had grown up with English comic books, nursery rhymes, and children's books; I was an Enid Blyton child. But apart from letters to my grandparents, I had never written in English; that, too, came from my time in Japan. But the main reason I chose London, I think, is that unlike Tokyo it was a city of many cultures.

Even though I decided to leave Japan, I knew that Japan would never leave me. I arrived in Tokyo when I was still unformed, callow and eager for experience. I can only hope that this eagerness will never be entirely dissipated. To be fully formed is to be dead. But Japan shaped me when the plaster was still wet.

There was another reason why Japan did not leave me. Sumie and I decided that home could be a moveable feast, as long as we were together. Soon after my break with Kara, I moved back in with her, in the same apartment we had rented when we first arrived in Tokyo. Just before leaving for London, she became my wife. She had come with me to the country of her birth, where she had always felt an outsider, and she would return with me to Europe, where she felt more at ease. Like Richie, she longed for radical autonomy. I shared that feeling. As the wise Indian writer Nirad C. Chaudhuri once said, to be *déraciné* is to be on the road forever. We were both gaijin for life. And we felt safer together.

When I told John Roderick, over lunch at the Foreign Correspondents' Club in Tokyo, that I was going to get married, he pulled a face of mild disgust. "How very, very boring," he said, as though I had finally sold out. He was wrong. It was never boring. The arrangement was not destined to last, but then one thing Japan had taught me was that nothing ever does. That is the sadness and the beauty of life.

We took off from Narita International Airport on a late autumn afternoon. I had hoped to get a last glimpse of Mount Fuji as we turned toward the ocean, but all I saw was a thick white blanket of cloud. My thoughts drifted to a boat trip I had once taken, not long after I first arrived in Japan, to an archipelago off the North Pacific coast celebrated by classical Japanese poets for its extraordinary beauty. Alas, on the day I set off to see the famous beauty spot, all the rocky little islands were shrouded in dense fog. There was nothing to be seen. But the tour guide, undeterred by reality, chirpily told us to observe the exquisite features of this island or that. Obediently, we looked left or right, as instructed, and sighed. The performance had to go on. We saw what we wanted to see.

Just then, the captain of our Japan Airlines plane announced that if we looked to the right, we could see Mount Fuji. We were sitting on the left, so I craned my neck to gaze across the row of seats, and there it was, the sharp outline of Fuji's proud cone, sticking out from the bed of clouds in all its glory. That was the last thing I saw of the country I had been living in for the last six years. I had been looking through the wrong window.

ACKNOWLEDGMENTS

I never kept a diary. And I wrote very few letters while living in Tokyo from 1975 till 1981. All I have to remind me of that period are photographs I took (none of myself; this was the pre-selfie age) and memories. Naturally, memories are fragmentary, fallible, and subject to constant change, as the story of one's life (never coherent in the first place) keeps being reedited in the mind.

All I can claim is that I have written this account of my Tokyo years as best as I can remember them. I have not consciously made anything up. But it is, for all the reasons mentioned above, as well as for literary purposes, an edited version.

I owe thanks to a few people who shared some of my experiences and were kind enough to jog my memory, above all Graham Snow and Rob Schipper.

Jim Conte, whom I first met in 1975 at the beautiful home of a mutual acquaintance in Kamakura, where he left an indelible and wholly misleading impression of impossible grandeur because of his ankle-length raccoon fur coat and plausible small talk about grand country houses, remained a friend for life. He was kind enough to read my manuscript. As was my wife, Eri Hotta, whose encouragement has been a constant spur to carry on.

ACKNOWLEDGMENTS

Jin Auh, of the Wylie Agency, saw the project through from beginning to end with her usual tact and moral support. And I couldn't have wished for more flexible, understanding, and professional editors than Scott Moyers and Christopher Richards.

INDEX

Note: Page numbers in *italics* refer to illustrations.

A NOTE ABOUT THE AUTHOR

Ian Buruma is editor of *The New York Review of Books*. He was educated in Holland and Japan and has spent many years in Asia, which he has written about in *God's Dust*, *A Japanese Mirror* and *Behind the Mask*. His other books include *The Wages of Guilt*, *Anglomania*, *Year Zero* and *Their Promised Land*.